BEFORE THE BLOOD TRIBUNAL

by

RUDI WOBBE & JERRY BORROWMAN

Utah Immigrant Survived Third Reich, But Not Cancer

The Salt Lake Tribune - reprinted by permission

Cancer killed him, but the disease was only one of many battles Rudi Wobbe fought during his life.

As a youth, he challenged the Hitler regime and for his crimes, spent $3^1/_2$ years in a Nazi concentration camp.

"He always spoke out on politics to make sure people don't sit idly by, that people are aware of what the government is doing and what's going on in the world," Karen Kadleck, Mr. Wobbes youngest daughter, said Tuesday. "He advocated being part of the political process right until his death."

Mr. Wobbe, 65, died Jan. 31 in a Salt Lake City hospital. At his funeral Tuesday, the machinist was heralded for his courageous battle against the cancer that afflicted his prostate, leg, and lungs during the last year.

But eulogies delivered Tuesday made little mention of an earlier battle—one he fought 50 years ago in Hamburg Germany, when Mr. Wobbe and two colleagues were accused of high crimes against the Third Reich

The three, members of the Resistance Movement, used Church of Jesus Christ of Latter-day Saints equipment and supplies to write anti-Hitler leaflets. The leaflets were placed in mailboxes, telephone booths, and in the pockets of coats hanging in an opera-house lobby. In the pamphlets they called Hitler a murderer and Nazis liars. They predicted the Nazis would be crushed.

Mr. Wobbe was 15 at the time. His friends, Karl Schnibbe and Helmuth Huebener were 16 and 17. Yet they understood the danger of their actions, for which they were caught, arrested and taken to the "Blood Court"—a room full of judges wearing blood-red robes.

The verdict: guilty.

Mr. Huebener's sentence was death under the guillotine blade, which was carried out.

Mr. Schnibbe drew a 5-year sentence. Mr. Wobbe got 10 years, but endured only $3^1/_2$ years of beatings by prison guards before being rescued by the Allies, the British.

The Wobbes found their way to Salt Lake City, world headquarters of their church. They arrived on July 4, 1953, "and have celebrated ever since," Mrs. Kadleck said.

But only in the last few years did Mr. Wobbe, whose heavy accent told of his German heritage, publicly speak of the fight for freedom that helped form his character.

"Even in church he was a loud, strong teacher; never boring. He'd bring out interesting points to stimulate people and challenge their minds," Mrs. Kadleck said. "Even his handshake was firm and challenging. He let you know he was a powerful man and commanded respect."

But no fanfare.

With prodding from family, Mr. Wobbe finally wrote about his life as a dissident. A week before his death came his greatest tribute. He signed a contract with Covenant Publishing to have his book *Before the Blood Tribunal* published.

Contents

CHAPTER ONE

GROWING UP IN GERMANY BETWEEN THE WARS

Perhaps the most remarkable thing about growing up in Hamburg, Germany, during the reign of the Nazis was how ordinary it seemed at first. Children playing, families at the park on Sundays, or young people going out for a movie were as much a part of our life as they were for people anywhere else in the world. In those days, neighbors talked a lot and our apartment complex was really a self-contained community with a diversity of views and opinions, but tempered by a camaraderie that I remember fondly, even now.

Of course there was the depression, which sometimes left my father unemployed, but Hitler convinced the Germans that their troubles were related to the unfair war reparations that the Allies demanded as their "spoils for winning the Great War." In fact, the greatest difference between Germany and the other nations of the world (who were struggling through their own economic hard times) is that Germany had someone to blame. In truth, the Allies had come down hard on the German people because of the overwhelming destruction they set in motion in the first truly "world" war. In an attempt to "civilize" Germany, they had forced the creation of the Weimar Republic, supported by a constitution that guaranteed personal liberties and freedom in much the same fashion as had become second nature to the citizens of the great democracies of the Allies. Unfortunately, once the Allied governments reached their conclusions and drafted their treaties, they left Germany on its own to find the way to self-rule and democracy—a project doomed to failure in a country that had been nurtured on the ideals of "duty to State above the individual," for many centuries.

In the early days, there was robust competition among the dozens of political parties that vied for power. Citizens felt free to fight for their causes and to attempt to have an influence on the government. In time, however, the battle increasingly became the Nazis versus everyone else. One of my earliest memories occurred one night as my parents were standing in front of our terrace apartment building talking with neighbors while we children played near by. Above our heads was a display from the Communist party, illuminated by a couple of spotlights. The communists stood nearby with materials to pass out to interested citizens. All of a sudden a car carrying a group of Nazis careened around the corner, brakes screeching. They stopped in front of us, jumped out and started beating up the people standing there, including innocent bystanders. Even we children felt the sting of their blows. During this unprovoked attack police stood by, doing nothing.

A month later there was a torchlight parade through our neighborhood. The marchers were from the Social-Democrat and Communist parties, but the Nazis, although uninvited, showed up too. They went atop the building across the street from us and stationed a machine-gun on the roof. While the demonstration was in full swing, they started shooting into the marchers, killing and injuring a number of them. The main body of marchers scattered quickly, but a group of them raced up the stairs after the Nazis and a battle ensued. Soon I saw the machine-gun and several bodies flying off the roof. With the Nazis thus disposed of, the marchers regrouped and the demonstration continued.

That same week, my parents and I were walking toward the streetcar stop at the Billhorner Roehrendamm when we came upon a car overturned in the middle of the street. Three men were hiding behind it with revolvers drawn, waiting for another car that was coming their direction. As soon as the car was close enough, the men started firing at it, causing the driver to make some wild maneuvers in an attempt to escape the rain of bullets. We children were so transfixed by this spectacle that we remained standing in the street. My father grabbed us and pushed us into the entrance of an apartment house nearby. It was all over in just a couple of minutes, but talk about excitement! Most people just shook their heads after it was over, and walked away. Others remarked how terrible the times were, while others cursed the Nazis for making it all happen. My father took me aside and said, "Son, don't ever get mixed up with those people, the Nazis. They are bad people!" My dad was a quiet man who never spent much time in idle chatter. Thus, when he spoke his message was usually profound. His words made a deep impression on me that day.

January 30, 1933 was a date that will live forever in history! The radio announced that Reichs-President von Hindenburg had just formed a new government, with Adolf Hitler as Chancellor. Hitler had persuaded the capitalist pressure groups and tycoons of industry that the only way they could work their way out of the depression was to bring the fiercely nationalistic Nazis into power. He promised to end the "tyranny of the Allied reparations" (which he did by inflating the economy to the point that he could pay off the Allies with worthless Reichsmarks), reestablishing Germany's "self-defense" capabilities (the factory owners were thrilled). The capitalists thought they would easily control Hitler for their ends. They failed to realize that his skills as an orator would soon allow him to control the masses through his rhetoric. He was a master at working the masses into a frenzy over the injustices that Germany had suffered and the humiliation they labored under because they were no longer a military power. The torchlight parades and patriotic rhetoric thrilled the Prussian blood that ran deep in German veins. Young men were so excited that they drilled with shovels instead of rifles, goose-stepping with right arm stretched out in the Hitler salute!

After Hitler was pronounced Chancellor, the Nazis really started flexing their muscles. Before this date they did their harassment of Jews and members of other parties under the cover of darkness. But in February and March of 1933, they brought their work into the daylight. I remember those days all too well.

Near our home was a shoe store, owned and run by a Jew. Even before 1933 his store windows had been broken and swastikas had been painted on the walls and door. But, after the "take-over," the Nazis demolished his store in broad daylight.

They broke all the windows, threw the merchandise onto the sidewalk, and dragged the proprietor and his wife and two children into the street. They started beating and cursing them all the while calling them dirty names and shouting that they weren't fit to live among the exalted German, Aryan people. The greatest indignity of all is that after the family was lying in the gutter in agony, the Nazis urinated on them. I was only seven years of age when this took place, but I still remember it vividly.

A couple of weeks after this incident, the Nazis had a big demonstration by torchlight down the main street of Rothenburgsort, the Billhorner Roehrendamm. They were marching twelve abreast toward the large open field which was later to become the building site for the Hanseatenhalle, or Hall of the Hanseatic League. Whenever the Nazi flag passed by, bystanders were supposed to salute the flag with the raised arm of the Hitler salute. It looked like everyone in the crowd was enthusiastically supporting the Nazis. What we did not see was that along the sides of the marching column were Storm Troopers who passed through the crowd. Whenever they spotted someone who was not properly saluting the flag, they swarmed on him and gave him a beating. I was standing in front of a group of people watching the parade with old Mother Schulz, who lived in our apartment building. When the flag passed by us she asked, "Rudi, do you see the color of that flag?" I replied that it was red. "No," she said, "it is the color of blood, and it is blood that they will spill!" This ominous statement always came back to my mind whenever I witnessed their atrocities later on. They even had the inscription, "Blood and Honor," engraved on their dress daggers. They used this distorted concept of honor to shed the blood of millions in the name of their leader, the Fuhrer.

Looking back, perhaps my life in Nazi Germany wasn't so ordinary, after all. But how can one know that the events one sees in everyday life are wrong or unusual without somehow gaining an outside perspective? After all, many of our neighbors were ardent supporters of the Nazis. In time, Hitler succeeded in putting the unemployed back to work and in rebuilding the nation's sense of honor and self-worth. Many influential citizens thought he was Germany's "savior," who would bring prosperity and help Germany take her "rightful place in the sun" (a quote that Hitler loved to use). In spite of the violence we saw from time to time, many felt that things were at last going right for our country. They were unable to see past the facade and understand the evil. If it hadn't been for my parents and my church, I may not have been able to gain a proper perspective either.

My father's chosen trade was boat building, but the depression had slowed the demand for the small luxury craft he built to the point where he couldn't make a living. He considered himself lucky to find a job at the Federal Control Commission for Brandy, where he labored as a dockworker and a maintenance man. The work was below his hard earned social status, but it provided an income to support my mother and me.

My father had been wounded in the First World War by a bullet which grazed his kidney as it passed through his body—a wound that caused him trouble the rest of his life. He often complained about feeling sluggish and tired. In early 1934 he was admitted to a hospital for treatment and seemed much improved for awhile. That summer we took a vacation on bicycles to visit relatives in Luebeck. It was a long, four-hour trip peddling up and down the hills. (I liked the downhill part best.) After establishing a "base camp" in Luebeck, our relatives joined us for another bicycle ride to Travemuende on the Baltic Sea. There we had fun swimming in the sea and lounging on the beach. I picked up jellyfish and threw them at my parents while they were in the water with me. We had a wonderful day and hated to go back to Luebeck that night. The days we were together went by too fast, like all vacations do, and it was soon time for the long journey back to Hamburg.

That turned out to be the last trip we would have with my dad. The next spring, on 6 March 1935, he passed away. I simply could not understand why he had to go—I still needed him and wanted to do so many things with him. I was just nine-years-old and felt a terrible loss. His death caused me to think seriously about life, even at that young age, and I went over his teachings in my mind many times. Among the lessons I had learned from my father were that all people are worthy of respect and dignity and that people should stand up for their beliefs.

My mother took my father's death hard, too. She told me that from then on I would be the man of the house and should look after her. I didn't understand the gravity of the situation at the time. My mom had to go back to work to take care of us. She got up at 3:00 A.M. to go to work cleaning offices. Later, she applied for a war veteran's pension, which was granted to her after six months. The amount was still too small to make ends meet, so she had to continue working.

On 7 June 1935, my mother and I were baptized into The Church of Jesus Christ of Latter-day Saints. My grandmother's missionary efforts had finally paid off. She was thrilled that another one of her children had joined her in the Church. As we became involved in Church activities, I formed friendships that would one day influence my thinking profoundly.

Since we lived in a predominantly reactionary neighborhood, filled with Social Democrats, Communists, and a few from the Iron Front, it was interesting to see many of our neighbors suddenly change their affiliations as the Nazis strengthened their stranglehold on political thought. It was common for a supposedly independent political thinker to suddenly show up in a Nazi uniform. The truth is, such people were either afraid to stand up for freedom, or they hoped for some economic gain by joining the Nazis. Some places of business were pressuring the workers to join up or leave. The Nazi ideology was taught in the schools and universities. Teachers who did not comply were suspended. The basic philosophy was that the worth of individuals was measured by their value to the whole, or more precisely, to the Nazi Reich. Individual freedom had to be sacrificed for the benefit of the Volk, or citizenry as a whole. The Nazi theme was emphasized over and over again, "Gemeinnutz Geht Vor Eigennutz." It means, "The common good is to be placed above an individual's requirements." An excerpt from a 1937 textbook illustrates how the Nazis sought to impress this concept onto the populace. The following is an example of eighth grade mathematics:

Question:

In 1936 the State Welfare Department provided 60, 530, 575 days of care to institutionalize the mentally ill, blind, deaf, dumb, and crippled.

Assignment:

1) Project the annual expenses for the above patients at a cost of RM 4.501 per day.

2) How high is the total annual expense to the District and State Welfare Departments?

3) Compare this enormous annual cost with a day's wages for a worker's time in a production factory. How many days of labor does it take to support these people if an average worker earns RM 3.20 per day?

4) How many workers, with 300 working days per year and an average income of RM 3.20, could a factory employ if the state didn't have the burden of supporting these people?

The Nazis were setting the stage for mass euthanasia at the basic school level!

In 1938 they came into the schools to Nazify the children. A group of Nazis, in full uniform, arrived one day in our school in Rothenburgsort. They set up tables in front of the class and asked each student to pass in front of the table. When it was my turn they asked if I was a member of the Hitler Young Folk. I said, "No, I am not."

"Why not?" they responded. "Are your parents Communists?"

"No, they are not," I replied.

"Well, what are you doing next Sunday," they then asked me.

"I am going to Sunday School," I told them.

"Oh, you are religious, are you?"

"Yes," I replied. "I believe in God and attend church."

"Do you have ten cents in your pocket for a membership fee?" the recruiter asked me. I told him I did not, but he said, "It doesn't matter. You are now a member of the Young Folk, anyway. You are to report for duty next Sunday at 10:00 A M." He then shouted, "Next," and I was dismissed.

I did not go to "duty" the next Sunday but went to church with my mother. A couple of weeks later, I met one of those leaders on the street, and he asked me why I was not coming to the meetings. I told him that I had other things to do on Sundays. He told me that I could also attend meetings on Wednesdays, and that it was a lot of fun there. I was curious, so went to the next meeting. There was a lot of camaraderie and group singing. But when they started demeaning the Jews by saying they were the curse of the world who stole from the German people and raped the German girls, I had the nerve to ask them for some proof. They started shouting at me, as if I were crazy. I did not go to any more meetings.

After that initial encounter they left me alone for awhile. The next summer they approached my mother, asking her to let me go to summer camp in Stolberg/Harz. We told them I couldn't go since I had no uniform. They offered to loan me one. With that I figured I had no way out, so I agreed to go.

I was very apprehensive about the whole thing, but at first everything went fine. Stolberg was a lovely little town with a lot of old medieval buildings set in rustic scenery. I didn't mind the marching and singing, but I had injured my knee while playing soccer and was excused on doctor's orders from any strenuous exercise. Some of the others thought I was just trying to get out of the military drill. Because of that and because of my reluctance to join in their bragging about what they were doing to the Jewish businessmen in town, I was left alone most of the time. I came to learn that I didn't fit into their group, and I felt uncomfortable there.

Whenever we had our political indoctrination sessions, I always spoke up when they attacked religious concepts. They started calling me the "Kirchenheini" (church clown). They made the most of the fact that I had different convictions. For example, I received a packet from home one day with some cookies and other goodies in it. I went off by myself to read Mom's letter and to enjoy some of the cookies. One of the leaders came by and pulled the packet from my hands, saying any packages from home had to be shared with the others. They handed my packet around the group, read my letter, and ate my cookies, handing me back an empty box. I was very upset and told them so in no uncertain terms. That night, after I'd fallen asleep, I was attacked by my tent "comrades" who administered the "Holy Ghost" by applying shoe polish garnished with toothpaste to my behind. The next morning they laughed as I tried to remove their artwork with soap, sand, and water. I couldn't wait for summer camp to end.

After returning home to Hamburg, I hurried to the party office to return the uniform they'd loaned me. They offered to let me keep it but I refused. I didn't want anything more to do with those people.

In the fall of 1939, Hitler ordered the invasion of Poland. After securing incredible concessions from the Allies through political negotiations, he at last stepped over the line into war. France and Britain declared war the next day, but could not move quickly enough to save the Poles, who were conquered by the German Blitzkrieg in a matter of weeks.

I was nearly fourteen when all of this was happening. In spite of the war, I ran errands for my mother and other people in the neighborhood. There was a woman living in a terrace nearby whose husband, a military policeman, was stationed in Poland. He sent home some photographs he'd taken of naked Jewish women and children who were lined up in front of an open pit with SS-troopers standing behind them, holding submachine guns. She laughed about those pictures and said how grotesque the naked women looked. I felt ashamed at her remarks and told her how calloused she must be to make fun of those poor people. "Those are not people," she said. "They are only Jews!"

"Are not Jews human beings who have just been robbed of their dignity?" I asked.

She responded caustically that "Jews have no dignity— they are lower than animals."

I was shocked, and told her so. I asked her not to call me again to run errands for her, because I didn't like her anymore.

In April of 1940 I graduated from school. My aptitude test had shown I was talented for metalwork. I wanted to be a boat builder, like my father, since he'd left me all his tools. Everybody tried to talk me out of it, though, because it was so seasonal in nature. They succeeded in steering me away from boat building and I started an apprenticeship in the H.F.C. Christian Bolte & Sons Steel Erections and Fabrications Shop. Since the war effort was going full blast, the work mostly consisted of fabricating U-Boat ladders and equipment. I was assigned to be a welder's helper and was errand boy for just about everyone under the sun. After a couple of weeks working there, I was assigned to replace some oxygen and acetylene bottles at the welding stations. Each bottle weighed 150 pounds, and while lifting one I ruptured myself. The doctor said I had to go into the hospital to have the hernia surgically corrected. After the operation I spent two weeks in a recuperation ward. While there I became aware of several men who had been admitted by the government for sterilization. They had some kind of hereditary illness, such as epilepsy, and weren't to have the privilege of fathering children. I was troubled that the government could make such an intrusion into the private lives and personal freedoms of the individual citizen.

After my recovery I returned to work only to be teased by the other apprentices and journeyman about being a "malingerer" who wasn't supporting the war effort. I was very much annoyed by this, but continued to do my job. One day it was my turn to shop for breakfast for the journeymen. I stopped by each worker to ask for his order. One particular welder refused to answer my inquiry and just kept on welding. I assumed he didn't want anything, so passed on to the next welder. What a mistake I made there! When I returned with the goods for the other men, he was waiting for me. He pounced on me screaming at the top of his voice that I had bypassed him when he was ready to give me his order. I reminded him that I had waited at his station, but had been ignored. He screamed that I was a liar and a religious idiot, and he swore violently. Then he started hitting me. A couple of the other journeymen tried to call him off, but he didn't listen to them. I put the food aside and started to defend myself. I was a pretty good athlete in school and had received some training in boxing. I blocked a couple of his punches but he kept coming, screaming obscenities at me all the while. Finally, I countered with my right into his solar plexus. He doubled over, and then I finished him off with an uppercut to the face. He went down for the count. The men cheered as I finished my rounds.

My enemy went to the Obermeister of the shop to report his side of the story. The Obermeister, in turn, called my mother in for a consultation. He told her he could not tolerate such impertinent behavior and that I should apologize to the injured welder. My mother rose magnificently to my defense. She told him that he had the story backward! It was her boy that had been attacked and beaten. She asked him what kind of a shop he was running that would allow apprentices to be beaten by ill-tempered journeymen. The Obermeister stood up, stretched himself to the full measure of his five and a half foot frame, and started to tell my mother what a rotten boy she had raised and that I was on the road to prison. My mother then stood up, and, finding that she was a few inches taller than he, looked down at him with all the dignity she could muster and said, "How dare you talk in this tone of voice to me. Who do you think you are, anyway? Do you think you are running a concentration camp here, where you can use my son as a whipping-boy? You better start cleaning up your shop by getting rid of these ruffians you have working for you!

"Furthermore," she roared, "I am a war-widow and deserve better respect from you. My son will no longer work in this archaic and obsolete place, and I will report you to the apprenticeship council so that they will remove this place from the list of desirable training shops."

I never before saw my mother in such a grand performance. She acted like a cornered lioness, defending her young. With that, she walked out of the office of the speechless Obermeister.

In June of the same year, I was advised to report to another place of work, the Norddeutsche Kohlen und Koks Werke, (North German Coal & Cokes Works), at the freeport center of the Hamburg Harbor. There I continued my apprenticeship. I found this a fascinating place to work because of its pumps and machinery that had to be maintained. The shop master was an old Social-Democrat who stayed true to his convictions. In fact, there were a lot of old-timers in this business who did not make the conversion to Nazism. When I entered the shop and greeted the men with "good morning," all but one replied, "Good morning, son." The other screamed, "Heil Hitler!" I knew right away where I stood with each of these people.

As the German army made its incredible march through Europe, the Civil Defense Department in Hamburg was busy building air raid shelters. Some of them were free-standing, round-shaped bunkers about four stories tall. Others were rectangular in shape, with concrete walls three feet thick. The shelters built in our area consisted of three large concrete pipes, eight feet in diameter, with connecting walkways. Construction of these shelters ruined the beautiful gardens located in the open areas between the buildings of our apartment complex. I played inside the bunker several times in order to become familiar with it. However, the army was so successful at this time that no one thought we'd ever need to use these shelters.

When I turned fourteen in the summer of 1941, the leaders of the local Hitler Youth started to harass me again. At my age young people were automatically transferred from the Jung Volk (Young Folk) into the Hitler Youth. I was attending an evening engineering school four nights each week, so there wasn't much time for anything else. One day I received notification to appear before a finding committee of the Hitler Youth. I took all my receipts and registration documents and visited the office. "Why have we not seen anything of you since you have been transferred to the Hitler Youth?" they demanded.

"I've been very busy going to school in the evenings after work," I replied, and showed them my papers. I went on to tell them I understood that the Fuhrer wanted the German youth to be the best educated in the world, and that's exactly what I was trying to do.

"Well, what about Sundays?" they asked. "Don't you have time then?"

I told them I didn't because I went to Sunday School with my folks, then. "Oh, you are one of those religious ones, are you?"

"Yes, I believe in God, and go to church on Sundays," I told them.

Out of the corner of my eye I noticed one of them get up and leave while we were talking, but didn't think anything of it. When I came out of the room he was waiting for me, wanting to "talk" with me. I told him I was in a hurry to go to school.

"Oh, you have enough time for me now," he blurted.

"What is it you want?" I asked him.

"We have our meeting scheduled right now, and you'd better attend it," he told me.

"I told you I am late for school, so you'd better let me pass," I said.

"No way. You have to stay." With that he started to push me against the wall.

"Hold it, man, you better watch what you are doing," I warned. "I don't like to be pushed around!"

"What are you going to do about it?" he asked, impertinently. "You can't touch me while I'm in uniform!"

"Then get out of it, you coward," I told him. He pushed me again, a little bit harder than the first time. By now I was getting angry, and while he was bending forward to push me again, I let him have an uppercut, which caught him square on the jaw. It knocked him out cold. I jumped on my bike and peddled at full speed out of the compound. Several weeks later I received another letter ordering me back to the office. This time I simply ignored it.

It was also in the summer of 1941 that my friend Helmuth Huebener told me his brother Gerhard had left him a short-wave radio for safe keeping. His brother had purchased it while on duty in France. Helmuth told me he had tried it out once, and he invited me to visit him at 9:30 P.M. that night, after his grandparents went to sleep. That meeting was to be a rendezvous with destiny and would change my life forever. At the tender age of fifteen I was about to embark on a course that would bring me in direct defiance of the Nazi government. But, first, we should go back in time just a bit to introduce you to my remarkable young friend, Helmuth Huebener.

CHAPTER TWO

MY FRIEND, HELMUTH

It was in Primary that I first met Helmuth Huebener. He was a shy nine-year-old and I was an exuberant eight-year-old. I was about half-a-head taller than Helmuth, but he towered over me in intelligence. He was a straight "A" student, while I managed only a good average. We found ourselves going to classes together, and in spite of our differences, we became fast friends.

Helmuth grew up in rather difficult circumstances. His mother was divorced and Helmuth was the youngest of three boys, his half-brothers coming from a previous marriage. To try to make ends meet, his mother had to work nights—first as a worker in the government mint, later at a local hospital. Because she was gone so much of the time, her parents, the Sudrows, agreed to take care of the children. Later, after Helmuth's mother married the Nazi Rottenfuehrer (minor official) Hugo Huebener, who adopted Helmuth, they asked if he wouldn't like to come live with them. Helmuth declined, saying that he liked living with his brothers and grandparents in their apartment on Louisenweg/Hammerbrook.

Helmuth and I liked to do the same things and read the same books. In the summertime I would visit Helmuth, and together we would go to an outdoor swimming area on the Bille River. Other times he came all the way to my home in Rothenburgsort to go with me to Kaltehofe, a swimming installation located on the Elbe River. We also enjoyed playing soccer and other games together with other boys our age.

Helmuth got me interested in reading books on world history. While I was still enthralled with the western novels of Zane Grey, Helmuth's interest shifted to politics and world affairs. A natural teacher, he would study a book and then pass it on to me pointing out key ideas I needed to take note of. After I had finished, he'd quiz me on the important points and the moral the author was trying to convey. He had great depth for one so young and had a remarkable ability to share his insights. It was because of this obvious ability that he was allowed to advance to the Oberbau (middle school) in 1938.

It was also this year that the Nazis entered my school to enroll everyone in either the Young Folks (Cub Scout age) or Hitler Youth (Boy Scout age), whether we wanted to join or not. Because he had always been fairly quiet on the subject of the Nazis, I assumed Helmuth would feel like most Germans—that it was an honor to be included. Still, I mentioned to Helmuth how much I resented being pushed into something against my will. Helmuth replied that the "Devil had tried to do the very same thing at the council in heaven before the world was formed, by putting forth a plan forcing everybody into salvation." This response surprised me, so I asked him how he felt about the Nazis. He replied, "Rudi, don't you ever believe what people are saying to you, especially in politics. They are always large in words but small in actions. Only time will tell," he went on, "because they are trying to win the working class over right now by providing employment and temporary economic gains."

"It sounds like you're not really sure of them," I said, to which he replied again, with a smile on his lips, "Time will tell."

Then I understood what he was trying to convey to me. He wasn't an ardent follower of Nazi ideology but was putting up a clever smoke screen so others could not see his real convictions and suspect his intentions. Pretty clever, I thought, and my respect for him grew even more.

Toward the end of 1938, Helmuth approached me with the idea of forming a detective agency. We had been reading the ten cent detective novels of authors such as John Kling and Rolf Torring. It was a real treat to read the twenty-five cent Lord Lister series. Because of our admiration for this heroic writer, Helmuth made up some identification cards that named us the Lord Lister Detective Agency. His badge number was #1 and mine was #2. He also wrote up some rules of conduct to govern our behavior as detectives.

We studied the police reports in the newspaper to find any unsolved crimes we could take on. After selecting a case, we tried to get some clues as to the Where? When? and Who Done It? questions that intrigue the curious mind. We even befriended one of the detectives from the local police station. Helmuth had such a way with people that this detective was soon very open with us.

He told us that a streetwalker had been stabbed to death in Rothenburgsort and asked us if we would snoop around to find the killer. For many nights we scurried about the streets of our area looking for anything suspicious. We kept running across a rather shady character by the name of Franz Seemann. He was a street bum who was always looking for a handout and free drinks. As we talked about it, we remembered seeing him in the company of the streetwalker in question just a few nights before her murder. We told this to the detective, and he pulled Franz Seemann in for questioning. Three days later we learned that he had confessed to the crime and that we had solved the case. Wow, did we feel great! With a solved mystery under our belts, we were true detectives—and we were only twelve years old.

Unfortunately, this was the only success we had. The other cases we took on were a lot more difficult, so after awhile we lost interest and drifted into other activities, but we still carried our ID CARDS, just in case.

Sometime later I cut my arm while jumping onto a windowsill that was about four feet above the ground. I had been showing off my athletic prowess but tripped and fell through the window. The glass broke, cutting a deep gash in my left wrist. The sight of blood gushing from the wound was enough to send me racing up the stairs to my mother. She wrapped a towel around my wrist and placed a tourniquet on the artery. She took me down to the grocery store and called a cab. At the hospital I was rushed to the emergency room. From there, I went straight into surgery, where they sewed the severed artery together again. When I awoke, I was startled to see two Gestapo agents standing by my bed to question me. When the doctor and nurses went through my pockets, they found my

Lord Lister ID CARD. That prompted them to call the Gestapo to report me as a potential enemy agent. The agents questioned me about the Lord Lister Detective Agency, asking what kind of a subversive organization it was and what foul goals this distinctively "English" organization had. Or, they asked, was it a cover-up for a secret underground movement? I was still groggy from the anesthetic and could not concentrate very well, but they kept pushing, trying to trip me up. I tried my very best to convince them that our "agency" was not a subversive or underground movement to overthrow the government, but just a game to be played by two innocent boys! After an hour they finally left me alone. But the incident wasn't entirely forgotten. A permanent file was made of the investigation.

The next year was an important one for the world. On 1 September 1939 the Second World War started with Germany's attack on Poland. Everybody was excited or scared. Helmuth grew very serious when I asked him how he felt about it. His response turned out to be prophetic when he replied, "The fire has started to burn—in Poland now—but soon the whole world will be in flames."

For me it was the last year I'd spend in school before starting an apprenticeship as a machinist. Helmuth had one more year left in the Oberbau. His greatest desire was to attend the university, but he knew it was unlikely he ever could.

"You have to have a rich father to attend the higher institutes of learning," he said. "So that leaves me out of the running." But he had great faith, and added, "I will not despair, for the Lord will find a way for me to continue my education."

This was Helmuth at his finest. He always managed to look on the bright side of life. His cheery disposition made it easy for him to find friends.

We attended the same Sunday School class, with Sister Eleanore Bremer as our teacher. She was a gracious lady who knew her lesson material by heart. We liked her a lot and had schoolboy crushes on her because she was very pretty and always wore sweet perfume. Because we liked her so much, we participated actively in class assignments. She rewarded us by giving us her old copy of the scriptures. She had purchased a new set for herself, but for us the old one was a real treasure.

As my friendship with Helmuth grew, we started discussing the lessons we learned from the scriptures. Helmuth was not afraid to tackle the hard parts of the gospel and wasn't at all shy in challenging uninformed adults if they didn't know the doctrine well. He sometimes asked the American missionaries such deeply thought out questions that he embarrassed them. They, in turn, would get a little gruff and tell him to leave things alone, that he was too young to ask such questions. Some adults even thought he was impertinent, but mostly Helmuth was just curious. It's true that he enjoyed rattling people's chains just a little. He just wanted to wake them up and make sure they were seeing all sides of a question. If Helmuth really wanted to though, he could have demonstrated a dazzling display of intellectual fireworks that would have outdistanced even the most educated of the brethren.

The year 1940 witnessed the first bombing raid over Hamburg. We heard that some bombs had fallen into St. Pauli, a section of Hamburg close to the harbor. After Sunday School the next weekend, Karl-Heinz Schnibbe and Helmuth joined me in a walk to the demolished section. When we finally arrived at Grosse Freiheit Street in St. Pauli, we found it difficult to make our way through the mass of people wanting to see the bombed-out house. One bomb had landed in the middle of the street, upturning the pavement and leaving a gaping hole where the street used to be. A second bomb had fallen onto a house, blowing away half its structure clear down to the first floor. We felt sorry for the people who had lost their home and belongings. Little did we know this was only the beginning of the massive destruction that would soon follow.

The war was building in intensity, but life went on in our neighborhood. One of the diversions we enjoyed was going to the movies together. But even there we couldn't escape the horrors of the Nazi world. On one occasion we went to a movie house where they played a German propaganda film entitled "Jud' Suess." The story was about a couple of Jews who were seducing and raping German girls. The movie, in a very demeaning way, portrayed the Jews as being a lecherous, grimy, and treacherous people. I was struck at how the Nazi propagandists preyed upon peoples' emotions through cunning and intrigue so they could gain control over them. Some in the audience applauded after the film, which really upset Helmuth. He asked, "How can people applaud something like this? How can they demean and dehumanize a whole race of people like that? Before the whole world the Nazis are depicting Germany as a nation of hateful and arrogant people. The Nazis proclaim to be such a super people, of Aryan and pure blood, but in reality they excel only in inhumanity and brutality."

Of course we saw other movies together that were fun to watch. Heinz Ruehmann starred in a hilarious comedy entitled, "Quax der Bruchpilot" (Quax, the Crazy Pilot). Laughter helped ease the tension of the war. But every so often Helmuth started talking about the "Jud' Suess" movie. The movie upset him for a long time.

In their attempt to control everything, the Nazis proclaimed any movie with dancing or kissing in it suitable only for those over the age of eighteen. Since my favorite movie star was a beautiful dancer, I didn't really like this restriction. Besides, since the party made the ban, we wanted to challenge it. The problem was getting past the Hitler Youth patrol who stood outside the movie to check ID CARDS. To outfox them we made it a point to dress sharply, wearing overcoats with white silk scarves and Hamburg hats, the kind successful businessmen or diplomats wore. In our disguise we usually fooled the Hitler Youth patrol so that they didn't ask for our cards.

Not long after the bombing raid in St. Pauli, the raids began in other parts of Hamburg. They made it necessary to have a volunteer air-raid watch in the buildings surrounding our church in St. George. Since our meeting house was part of a larger warehouse complex, we had to post a fire watch as well. Helmuth, Karl-Heinz, and I were asked to fill this watch on New Year's Eve, 1940. At the last minute, Karl-Heinz found a party to go to, so he begged off and Arthur Sommerfeld took his place. The adult assigned to watch with us was Heinrich Worbs, our old friend. I brought some games to play, and Helmuth brought a radio. We didn't play many games because Heinrich Worbs told us stories about growing up in the Hamburg harbor as well as ghost stories that kept us sitting on the edge of our chairs. At midnight all the church bells throughout Hamburg started ringing and the ships in the harbor sounded their foghorns and steam whistles. Fireworks were prohibited because of the war, but some people set off fireworks anyway. We ascended six stories to the roof of the warehouse to take in the festivities. The night wasn't as grand as the celebrations before the war, but somehow the people of Hamburg seemed to have a good time in spite of war restrictions. In fact, they weren't really very obedient to party rules. Even dancing was officially prohibited, but not many paid attention.

After the noise subsided, we went back down to our watch room again to have some Gluehpunsch (hot cider) and some berliner pfannkuchen (bismarks) which my mother had baked for us. Before we had the refreshments, Brother Heinrich Worbs asked us all to kneel down and have a word of prayer. With a mighty voice he asked the Lord to give us peace, to break the yoke of the Nazi butchers, to make us free, and to prosper the cause of Zion in Germany. He also prayed for the leaders of the Church that they might have the spirit of Christ in their hearts and with love lead the flock into all righteousness despite the prevalent Nazi influence. After the prayer, we looked at each other, and together cautioned Brother Worbs to be more careful of what he was saying in public.

"I tell the truth and nothing but the truth, and I cannot tell a lie," he replied.

"We understand this and agree with you, but please be careful who you are talking to," we urged him. (About a year later, we had occasion to remember this sad warning when our friend was arrested by the Gestapo for making a derogatory remark on the street one day about the Nazis.)

During a lull in the conversation, Helmuth started to play with the dials of the radio, trying to tune in a station other than those authorized by the German Reich. He succeeded in getting Radio Basel/Switzerland and Radio Liechtenstein, but that was all he could find. Every couple of hours we had to go through the warehouse on our routine watch cycle, but everything was all right. There weren't even any air raids to break up the evening. As morning approached, we went to bed to get some sleep. Heinrich Worbs stayed up to read the scriptures, kidding us when we were unable to keep our eyes open anymore. Finally, at 6:00 A.M. our relief came.

Sunday morning and evening were spent in Church services, and Church activities kept us pretty busy during the week. On Monday evening the men went to priesthood meeting while the women attended Relief Society. On Wednesday, the young men and women attended the Mutual Improvement Association, while the Boy Scout age group attended the Juniors (the Boy Scouts had been disbanded by the government in favor of the Hitler Youth). On Friday, to close the week out, we had choir practice.

After these meetings, we would all walk home together. When we reached the Hammerbrookstrasse, Karl-Heinz would break away and travel toward Hohenfelde. The rest of us would continue on toward Hammerbrook, talking, laughing, and singing together. Most of the time we liked to sing hymns but occasionally would sing American songs the missionaries had taught us, such as "You Are My Sunshine" or "Moonlight and Roses." Helmuth particularly liked to sing the American songs. One day, as we were happily singing away, a Hitler Youth patrol stopped us and demanded that we let them inspect our identification cards. After looking them over, they demanded to know why we were singing English songs.

"They are not English songs, but American," Helmuth smarted off. "And why shouldn't we sing them?" he added. "It's not against the law!" With that he really warmed to his subject and said, "Talking about the law, what right do you think you have to harass German citizens on the street? You've not been given the authority of a policeman to question people!" So intense was Helmuth's tirade that the members of the youth patrol were effectively confounded. Finally they gave up and withdrew, unable to compete with Helmuth. After they left, Helmuth said, "That is the trouble with these people—put them in a uniform and they think they have the authority to bully people around. It doesn't matter whether they belong to the Hitler Youth, the SA, or the SS. But that's the way the whole system has become. Our country is being run through threats, intimidations, and even brutal force! And something has to be done about this!" Helmuth's steps had become shorter and shorter as he talked. Finally, he stopped with his eyes fixed on a distant spot in the road.

After a moment, I touched him on the shoulder and said, "Helmuth, is there something the matter with you?"

He bolted, as if being awakened from a deep sleep, looked at me and said, "Yes, something should be done about this!"

"What, Helmuth?" I asked him.

"Not now, Rudi. Not just yet, but soon."

I let it go, but had a feeling he was up to something. To break the serious mood, I said, "Helmuth, let's do some more singing and forget those uniformed party slaves who tried to spoil our evening."

"Yes," he replied, "let's sing." And with this he started an exuberant rendition of "Moonlight and Roses." We all fell in with the song, and pretty soon the dark feeling dissipated.

We parted company and I continued to Rothenburgsort alone. During that quiet walk, I found myself in deep contemplation. I'd seen a different Helmuth than I'd known before. For the first time I had seen deep into his soul. I was intrigued by his intense, negative feelings for the Hitler Youth and the party system. His comment that "something should be done about it," let me know that some kind of resolve was building in his mind. It was also apparent he wasn't yet ready to convert his thoughts into action. No matter how I tried to characterize the remarkable events of that night, I couldn't help but feel that something extraordinary was going to happen and that Helmuth would be in the middle of it. I sensed it would be dangerous and felt both fear and excitement.

The next time we met I asked again what he was up to, but Helmuth just said, "Later, Rudi." Helmuth did tell me of something he'd just read by Heinrich Mann, one of the authors banned by the Nazi Party. The title of the book was *Geist und Tat* (Spirit and Action). As always, he was trying to teach me about political systems by letting me know about the problems other people and nations faced that were similar to Germany's. In the book, Mann quoted Napoleon as saying, "Revolutions are rare, because human life is too short. Everybody thinks to himself, 'it will not profit me to upset the existing order, so why bother?'" Mann went on to say that while the French revolution, with its stirring battle cry, "Liberty, Equality, and Fraternity," echoed throughout the world, those grand aims were forgotten as the bourgeoisie and nobility quietly reestablished themselves. Helmuth said that Mann felt it would be even more difficult to bring about a revolution in Germany because the German people are so fatalistic. While they are deep thinkers who love philosophy, they have a deep suspicion that there really is no great meaning or purpose to life. Thus, they seek security above all else and are unwilling to overthrow a bad government because of the attitude, "What difference would it make anyway?" Hence, Helmuth concluded, the people were willing to accept Hitler because, in some perverse way, he managed to create for them a fatal feeling of safety.

This was just one example of the deep conversations Helmuth and I had on politics. Because he had received straight A's on his final examinations and dissertation on graduation from basic school, he had been given the high honor of going on to middle school. He was also given a job as an intern to the Department of Social Services. In this position he was being trained to one day hold a career as a high government official. One of the benefits of working there was that most of the books banned by the Nazis were stored in the building archives. This allowed Helmuth to occasionally sneak out books for us to read.

Looking back across the years, I see how much I enjoyed my discussions with Helmuth. With each book he read, his brilliant young mind was resolving itself to the fact that the Nazi regime was evil and should be resisted. Because Helmuth had a strong sense of right and wrong, he felt compelled to explore ideas outside the narrow scope of government propaganda. That intellectual curiosity, coupled with his deep religious conviction of the basic value of each of God's children, was leading him on a collision course with the Nazi Reich.

CHAPTER THREE

CONTEMPT FOR THE NAZI REGIME

Every family needs a physician. Ours was Dr. Loewenberg, a splendid doctor and surgeon. He was the one who treated my childhood bouts with mumps, tonsillitis, and chicken pox. His good reputation in the medical community and with his patients was probably the reason the Nazis left him alone as long as they did. You see, he was a Jew.

One day the inevitable happened. We approached his office for an appointment only to find a Storm Trooper blocking the door. My mother asked the meaning of this. The Storm Trooper emphatically replied, "No German citizen would willingly patronize a Jewish doctor, and I am here to prevent it!"

"But *we* do!" said my mother, as she pushed the Storm Trooper aside to enter the building. But the next time we tried to visit Dr. Loewenberg things didn't work out so well. Instead of a Storm Trooper, we were greeted by an empty office with a sign posted saying, "Der Jude ist raus!" (The Jew is out!) That was the last time we ever saw the good doctor.

However, a few weeks later we noticed his office was again occupied by another physician named Dr. Maack. Upon entering, we couldn't help but notice the jackboots and the black uniform of the SS hanging from the coat hanger in his office. We didn't visit him again.

More and more frequently, neighbors were disappearing from our apartment building. The Nazis made certain everyone could hear the commotion they created while arresting one of the terrace residents. The next day we would all ask, "Who was picked up last night?" Then, one or the other of the children would reply, "My father was arrested by the Gestapo!" The two most common reasons for such arrests were opposing the party program or supporting the Jews. There were a lot of former Communists and Social Democrats living in our neighborhood which made it a prime target for the Nazis.

Of course these weren't the only reasons one could be arrested. If you were too frequently late for work or if you didn't get along well with the party representative, you were reported as an "antisocial" individual in need of rehabilitation at a concentration camp. If, by chance, you asked for a couple of days of leave of absence for personal reasons, you were branded an "idler" or "lazy worker," which called for corrective training. If your boss didn't like you or wanted to get even with you for some reason, all he had to do was report you to the Gestapo, and you were picked up and sent to a concentration camp for a stern dose of "work education." The party never talked about what went on in the concentration camps, but one look at a returning victim told us how awful it was. Another "sin" that earned you a ticket to a concentration camp was allowing someone to overhear you complain about the war or the twelve-hour day you were forced to work. Such expressions stamped you as a "defeatist" in need of an attitude change. The worst crime of all was to openly oppose the Nazis by belonging to another party, such as the Communists, Social Democrats, Free Liberals, or Christians. Anyone who did not give up his former affiliations and join the Nazis was in danger of being declared a political enemy, marked a "Political," and promptly sent to a concentration camp.

We learned about the horrors of the concentration camps first hand from a member of our congregation, Brother Heinrich Worbs. We knew him to be a devout Christian, a simple but honest man. His only fault was that he always said what he was thinking and feeling at the time. Among friends that was okay because we would keep his remarks to ourselves. One day, while watching the Nazis erect a statue of one of their "Nazi-heroes," Heinrich remarked, "Another statue for one of those Nazi butchers!" He was overheard and reported to the Gestapo who immediately arrested him and shipped him to Neuengamme, a feared concentration camp near Hamburg. They kept him for six months. After being released he attended Church meetings again, but we could hardly recognize him. He was a broken man, a shadow of his former self. Brother Otto Berndt took him under his wing and slowly nurtured him back to where he could at least carry on a conversation. When Helmuth and I had a chance to question him privately, he told us that he was not allowed to talk about the treatment he had received. Indeed, he'd been forced to sign a paper that said he was simply there for educational purposes and had been treated well. Further, his captors threatened that if he ever said anything to the opposite effect, he would immediately be returned to the concentration camp and would never be released again.

All the time he was telling us about this he was shaking violently as a leaf for fear that they might get him again. Eventually, we calmed his fears to the point that he could tell us what had happened to him. The story sickened us. It seems that part of the "reeducation" process was to force the prisoners to stand naked, or nearly so, outside in the middle of the winter, ankle deep in snow, with their hands shackled together. To make things worse, the SS would pour water over their shackled hands, which soon turned to ice. Then they would come by and beat on the frozen hands with a rubber hose or stick to "warm" them up. While telling us of his ordeal, poor Brother Worbs was constantly looking from side to side, afraid that someone might take him back. We were appalled at the treatment he had received and of the frightened, beaten wreck they had made of this gentle soul. Six weeks later he died.

What upset Helmuth and me most was the way the other members of our congregation treated Brother Worbs upon his return. Rather than rally to his defense to comfort him, many turned a cold shoulder, refusing even to speak with him. He was ostracized because he "kicked against the pricks," by opposing the government. Many, I suspect, were afraid to be seen with him for fear the Nazis would suspect them as well. Thus was the mighty party able to enforce its iron hold on the citizens. By crushing one man, they could terrify everyone else into quiet submission.

Probably the easiest way to gain admittance to a concentration camp was to be a Jew. Anti-Semitism raged throughout prewar Europe. The Germans were not alone in prejudice against this race of people. But, it was only through the un- limited dictatorial powers of Adolf Hitler that six million peo- ple would be subjected to his "final solution." In his cold and calculating way, he set in motion the machinery to attempt to destroy an entire race from off the earth. Only total military defeat was able to quiet this monstrous machine, which had grown drunk on blood and terror.

Under the guise of maintaining racial purity, the Nazis first deprived the Jews of their property and employment. Next, they were herded into crowded corners of the major cities, called ghettos. The ghettos, in turn, fed the furnace of the holocaust as families were torn apart to be sent to the con- centration camps where execution or terrible deprivation and inhumanity awaited.

Hitler wasn't just interested in eliminating the German Jews. Whenever a country was conquered, the SS made a sweep through the population to search out the Jews and deport them. Even the half- and quarter-blood Jews were harassed—espe- cially if they were married to Aryan spouses. When they found such a mixed marriage, the SS "requested" the Aryan to divorce the Jew. If they refused to abandon their spouses, they were charged with violation of the Racial Purity Law, which meant non-Jewish spouses would lose their employment. For the rest of the war they were required to perform menial jobs, such as janitor, regardless of professional training or education. One day I found a former department store manager sweeping the floors in the same building he used to manage.

There was simply no end to the lengths the Nazis would go to humiliate a Jew. I saw a Jewish man paraded through the streets of Hamburg with a sign hung around his neck that said, "I am in town the greatest swine, for only with German girls do I sleep and dine."

One of our friends at church was a very intelligent young man named Salomon Schwarz. He was born in Balagansk in Siberia, Russia on 2 July 1916. His mother was a Hungarian Jew who was abducted by the Russians and deported to Siberia in World War I. On the way there, she was raped by a Russian soldier. In this act, he fathered Salomon.

While in Russia, she met and married German prisoner-of- war, Hermann Schwarz. Salomon's maternal grandparents, the Lehrers, were well to do and sent money to buy their POW son-in-law's way out of Russia. With this help the family was able to return to Hamburg, Germany. Here Salomon grew through the years of childhood as a member of his stepfather's Protestant church. About the time he turned eighteen, he started to ask many questions which his church couldn't answer. His search ultimately led him to the Church of Jesus Christ of Latter-day Saints, which he joined on 7 June 1935. He was very enthusiastic about his new church and helped in the conversion of his half sister, Anna Marie. He and Anna Marie belonged to the Barmbeck Branch of the Church, which was presided over by my future father-in-law, Alfred Schmidt. They were very content in their Church associations until an unhappy incident occurred in early 1939.

Because the Barmbeck Branch had a very small meetinghouse, whenever a large group needed to meet everyone would travel to our building, the St. Georg Branch, because it had a larger meeting hall. Salomon had joined the district choir, which practiced each Friday evening at the St. Georg meetinghouse. Somehow, the branch president at St. Georg became suspicious of Salomon and one day confronted him. He demanded that Salomon produce an Aryan ID CARD, which, of course, he was unable to do. The branch president told him not to visit the branch again until he could prove he was an Aryan. Shortly thereafter a sign appeared on the entrance to the Church that said, Jews Are Not Allowed To Enter! This was directed against Salomon and others of mixed-blood lines. Because the Church had always taught the importance of tolerance for people of all races, some of the local brethren objected to the placing of such an un-Christian sign on the door of the branch meetinghouse.

When confronted, the St. Georg branch president simply said, "I am just following party lines." He'd been a member of the Nazi party since 1933. It should be noted that this was the only meetinghouse in all of Germany that had such a sign placed above its door. Needless to say, Salomon was shocked and devastated. He did not expect this in what he considered to be the true church. He went to his own branch president, Alfred Schmidt, who assured him that he was always welcome in the Barmbeck Branch and would never be greeted by such a sign there.

Salomon then told his troubles to his friend Walter Schmidt, who went right to work trying to help him. Walter wrote a letter to the Reichssippenamt (Racial Control Office), forwarding a signed affidavit stating that Salomon was of non-Jewish character and stature. This document was signed by friends of Salomon's, including members of the Nazi Party. They were all hoping that Salomon would be classified like the rest of his brothers and sisters, who were identified as half Jews. With this designation, they were not required to wear the six cornered Star of David, which proclaimed the bearer as a Jew. Without the star, they were not harassed and could move about freely. Such were the hopes that inspired the letter. But, the Reichssippenamt failed to reply.

While awaiting an answer, Salomon hoped he would be able to attend a special Church conference meeting at the St. Georg meetinghouse which was featuring a visiting speaker. As they approached the meeting, he asked his sister to go inside and ask permission from the mission president for Salomon to attend. The president sent a message out with his secretary that Salomon would not be able to enter. His sister, with a heavy heart, had to go and tell him of the decision. Salomon broke down and cried as he said, "Why can't I be with my brothers and sisters in the gospel and worship with them?" His sister told him to go home, assuring him she would report the messages of the conference to him later. He told her he wanted to stay there, outside the chapel, to hear the Church hymns they were singing.

It was two years later, in 1941, that Salomon thought he could get an answer if he would apply directly in Berlin to the Reischssippenamt. Before he left on his journey, the whole membership of the Barmbeck branch knelt down in prayer in his behalf. While he was in Berlin to plead his case, a party member reported to the Gestapo that Salomon was not wearing the Star of David. Legally he wasn't required to wear the Star, since his case was still pending. But as soon as he returned from Berlin he was arrested by the Gestapo and shipped to a concentration camp for "educational purposes." His clothing was sent home to his mother. After carefully opening the bundle, she noticed some blood stains on it and screamed loudly, "What have they done to my boy?"

After three weeks they released Salomon. As he came through the door of his home he collapsed and fell into a coma. The family was unable to revive him. His sister Anna Marie rushed to get their branch president, Brother Schmidt, to help him through the power of faith and the priesthood. When she got there, she found that Ernst Schmidt, a son, was also there on furlough from the army. He offered to help and all three immediately began the one hour walk to Salomon's house. Upon arriving, they anointed his head with consecrated oil and blessed him by the power of the priesthood with the instruction to arise. Salomon opened his eyes and sat up. He was very weak and in need of spiritual comfort even more than physical sustenance. They did their best to raise his spirits through cheerful conversation.

When it came time for the two brethren to leave, Salomon pleaded with them to stay and pray with him. They did, hoping all the time that no air-raid alarm would sound to disturb them. It was early morning the next day when Salomon finally calmed down enough to go to sleep. Only then, did they leave for their own homes.

Shortly after this Salomon had to appear before the Nazi court to learn of the findings of the Reichssippenamt. He was still too weak to make it on his own, so Ernst Schmidt, in army uniform, went with him. As Ernst helped Salomon to the witness box, the judge challenged Ernst, saying, "Aren't you ashamed to associate yourself with this Jew, thus soiling the uniform of the German Soldier?"

Ernst replied, "I don't see a Jew, your honor. I only see my friend!" But, the finding of the high office was that Salomon was a full-blooded Jew and would be required to wear the Star. The reasoning behind the decision was that Salomon's Russian father must have been a Jew, since only a Jew would touch a Jewish woman. It was through this clever reasoning that Salomon was found to be one hundred percent Jewish. The Nazis added "Israel" as his middle name (as they did all declared Jews) and sentenced him to move into the ghetto, in the Benekestrasse/Grindel. Before his move, the family had to put a sign on their door declaring that a Jew lived there. It was during this time that Brother Otto Berndt, then district president of the Church, visited Salomon regularly to give him comfort and support. After his move to the ghetto, it was

Walter Schmidt who visited him, even though it was strictly forbidden for an Aryan to visit a Jew. In spite of warnings that he too could be sent to a concentration camp, Brother Schmidt valued his friend's needs more than his own safety and went anyway. He had faith that he was on the Lord's errand and would be protected. His faith was justified.

Salomon stayed in the ghetto until 12 February 1943. On that day he was transported to Auschwitz, where he died in the gas chambers.

While the Nazi party never officially condemned the Christian churches of the country (Hitler didn't want that problem on top of all his others), they undermined the meaning of Christianity by slowly replacing men's allegiance to God with loyalty to the party. For example, the same branch president who caused Salomon so much trouble reprimanded an elderly sister in our branch. On the way to Church one Sunday morning, she had stooped to pick up a leaflet dropped by the British onto the streets of Hamburg. When she arrived at the church she casually showed it to some of the other members. When the president saw what she was doing, he ripped the leaflet from her hand and started shouting, "If you ever bring enemy propaganda literature into this branch house again, I will see to it that you are brought into a concentration camp!"

This action disturbed me deeply. Just two weeks earlier our Sunday School teacher, Sister Bremer, had taught a marvellous lesson about Jesus' instructions to his disciples and the importance of the first and second commandments—to love God with all your heart and soul and to love your neighbor as yourself (see Matthew 22:36–40). I also thought of the scripture where the Lord differentiated between the righteous and the unrighteous when he said, "Inasmuch as ye have done it unto one of the least of these my brethren, ye have done it unto me" (Matthew 25:40). Somehow I couldn't shake the image of our branch president threatening one of his flock with deportation to a concentration camp simply for picking up a leaflet. When I told Helmuth of the incident, he grew very serious and said, "The evil influence of Nazism, with its disregard of human rights and feelings, is making inroads even into the Church by changing people's priorities and loyalties." Here again, I was taken aback by the depth of his thinking.

As we continued this discussion, we talked of the growing role of the party programs in the Church. For example, we often had to respond to the invitation to listen to the speeches of Hitler or Goebbels during our youth activity night before we could get on with the social activities planned for the evening. Each time the branch president conveniently provided a radio so there would be no excuse to not listen.

The influence of politics on our Church activity got to the point that it seemed to us many of our Christian brothers and sisters considered Hitler to be the "savior of Germany." Superficial parallels were drawn between the Nazi party and the Church, including its organizational structure and strong emphasis on the active participation of every member. Even the fact that the LDS Church encourages genealogical research seemed to coincide with the Nazi's demand for rigorous genealogical pedigrees that proved one's Aryan ancestry. In an attempt to coexist with the Nazi government, American Church officials resorted to public relations efforts which suggested all of the above. The most outspoken Church leader was the East-German Mission President, who published an article in the Nazi newspaper, *Der Voelkische Beobachter* (*The People's Observer*), implying that it was the responsibility of Church members to actively support their government. Dated 14 April 1939, this article caused many in the Church to feel Hitler's cause was justified. Some even included him in their public prayers, asking for divine guidance in his behalf.

Similar incidents were taking place in other churches throughout the land. Of course there were many courageous church leaders who spoke out against the Nazi's rule, but they soon wound up in concentration camps.

The Nazi's covert campaign against religion created a great dilemma for God-fearing citizens. The demands of government often intruded on the traditional goals of organized religion, such as support for one's neighbor, respect for the rights of individuals, etc. When there is a conflict between them, where does one's loyalty lie—with God or government? That was the great question for us.

In retrospect, I can't say what all the precise annoyances were, but it wasn't long before Helmuth Huebener, Karl-Heinz Schnibbe, and I found ourselves united in a growing dissatisfaction with Nazism. There were simply too many contradictions to reconcile. During the day we listened to the propaganda about Hitler and his party helping the German people reestablish their "place in the sun," while at night they came and arrested the fathers and mothers of our friends. If the party was so great and benevolent, why should it be so frightened of dissent or free thinking? Yet, they punished even the slightest opposition.

In Church it was always Helmuth who spoke up, debating the issues. Sometimes he walked the narrow line, challenging the elders to stand up and be counted. He was told to be quiet, that he was too young to understand these things. Whenever the party members tried to subdue our thinking by reciting the long list of Nazi accomplishments, we'd think of Emerson's famous statement, "What you are doing thunders so loudly in my ears that I cannot hear what you are saying." As we watched in disgust at the great injustices being done to our neighbors and fellow Church members, our irritation grew into anger. The actions of the Nazi party and its faithful followers contradicted everything we felt to be noble and sacred. As we watched Salomon Schwarz pass through his Gethsemane, our anger grew into a quiet resolve to do something to resist the evil that now dominated our land.

CHAPTER FOUR

PREPARATION TO HIGH TREASON

Our story has now come back to the summer of 1941. A victorious German army had swept through Europe, gobbling up Austria, Czechoslovakia, Poland, Norway, Denmark, the Netherlands, Belgium, and France. Current battles were being fought in the distant lands of North Africa, Yugoslavia, and Greece. The German people were proud of their seeming invincibility.

Then, on 22 June 1941, Hitler made one of the most momentous decisions of the war—he ordered the invasion of Russia. In spite of his infamous Nonaggression Pact signed with Stalin just days before the invasion of Poland, he now repudiated the pact and turned his eyes to the east. Everyone assumed the German army would meet with the same success in this endeavor as they had on all the other fronts. German youth marched by torchlight, shouting salutes to their Fuhrer. Things were going well for Adolf Hitler in 1941. He was a winner, and few Germans dared to defy him.

Among the few who did were we three young men of Hamburg who had at last had enough. Even at the tender age of fifteen, the innocence of youth had disappeared, lost to the cruelty of the Nazi party. We were now young men who felt capable of independent thought and action. Our resistance started when Helmuth's half brother, Gerhard, came home on a furlough from the Western front. While there, he purchased a Rola shortwave radio which he left with Helmuth for safe keeping. Of course it was impossible for anyone as naturally curious as Helmuth to not explore this delightful wonder. As he searched the airwaves, his excitement grew. For the first time in years, he was able to tune into the world outside the German realm. As if guided by fate late one evening he turned into a broadcast by the British Broadcasting Corporation (BBC). He started to listen to it regularly. He was so thrilled with what he was hearing that he had to share it with me as soon as possible. I'll never forget the first night I heard this remarkable broadcast. I arrived at about 7:00 P.M. and talked with his grandparents for awhile. As usual they went to bed early, saying good night to us and asking me to not stay too long. For awhile, we perused some of the forbidden books that Helmuth had borrowed from the Social Services library. Finally, at 10:00 P.M., it was time for the broadcast to begin. With our ears glued to the receiver we heard the first bar from Beethoven's Fifth Symphony, "Did did did dah—This is BBC London with the German news broadcast!" (As of the beginning of the war, 1 September 1939, a law had been passed that forbade all citizens to listen to any foreign broadcast. But this didn't bother us, for we wanted to know what was happening.)

There was a vast difference between the news the BBC gave us versus the Wehrmachtsbericht (Armed Forces News) and the German newspapers. BBC London gave the casualties precisely for both sides—not at all like a typical German news report, which sounded something like this, "Massive casualties were inflicted upon the Russian Army, with relatively few losses for our own victorious troops." Another broadcast that amused us was a report on the success of the Luftwaffe in sinking the British aircraft carrier, the Ark Royal. According to the BBC, she was still afloat. We heard the same report on another occasion. Helmuth told us later the Germans had sunk this poor ship three different times. The British stood by their story that she remained undamaged and very much battle ready.

At the end of each broadcast, the BBC would invite its listeners to find others who would tune in, then give the times of rebroadcasts. Helmuth hurriedly wrote these down in shorthand. I asked him when he'd learned to take shorthand. "Oh, I took a couple of classes in school," he replied. "Things like shorthand and typing, really come in handy." I was about to find out just how handy his typing skills were.

The next time we met, he gave me a handbill, about one-fourth the size of a sheet of typing paper and asked me to read it. Entitled "Hitler the Murderer!" it contained the message we'd heard on the previous radio broadcast. It talked about the murder of General von Schroeder, military commander of Serbia. I told him the pamphlet looked great, particularly since it was printed on red paper. "Then let's go to work," Helmuth replied. He handed me a stack of leaflets and said, "Put them in mailboxes, telephone booths, and other places—be inventive." But, Rudi," he went on, "be careful not to let anyone see you."

With that, I took off. When I arrived back in Rothenburgsort's Billhorner Roehrendamm, which runs parallel to the Hardenstrasse where I lived, I went to the top floor and started to drop off the handbills in the mailboxes (strasse translates to "street" in English). I quickly learned that I had to be very quick, so people wouldn't see me. Whenever I came out of an apartment house, I kept close to the building so no one could look out and see me from above. Proceeding with this method of distribution, I covered about three apartment houses before my supply ran out. I distributed about thirty to thirty-five handbills that first night.

The following Sunday I reported my success to Helmuth and told him everything had gone all right. He told me he had a new batch of handbills ready for delivery. The titles were, "Hitler Is Guilty of the Bombing Raids Over Germany!" and, "Who Is Lying?" a pamphlet that compared the Wehrmachtsbericht reports with the news from the BBC. I distributed these new pamphlets in the Markmannstrasse, Kanalstrasse, and Lindleystrasse in Rothenburgsort. I was interested to find that the Nazi Party had placed bulletin boards at the entrance of every apartment house in the area with the intriguing title, "Bulletin Board of the N.S.D.A.P." (in other words, the Nazis' public bulletin board). I couldn't resist the challenge and placed our new handbills on those boards, as well.

It took a real effort on Helmuth's part to produce the leaflets. His system worked something like this:

1) He'd listen to a BBC broadcast, taking down key points in shorthand.

2) After transcribing his notes, he'd decide whether to

copy the broadcast verbatim or use it as a basis for writing an article in his own style.

3) Once the article was prepared, he used our church typewriter to produce the leaflets on bright red paper for distribution. As clerk for our local congregation, he'd been given use of the typewriter to write letters to servicemen in the field. Usually he'd prepare sixty quarter-page leaflets. By using five carbons, he "only" had to type the message twelve times. When he prepared the full-page dissertations, the task was even greater.

4) He did the typing late at night, after his grandparents had gone to bed. He chose to use red paper because it drew attention to the message. To throw the Nazis off the track, he always drew a big, black swastika in the corner. Thus, the casual observer would assume it was just another party bulletin. What a surprise awaited the person who took a closer look.

Over time, Helmuth wrote many different handbills and dissertations, which his small network distributed throughout the city. We did what we felt was right in trying to bring truth to our neighbors. The German Government saw it as the beginning of the crime of Preparation to High Treason. We didn't realize, of course, how famous our activities would soon make us. But, Helmuth didn't hold anything back. He was determined to reveal the truth hidden behind the propaganda. Here is a sample of some of the handbills:

1. Hitler Is Guilty: Of the Bombing Raids Over Germany.

2. Hitler the Murderer: Of General von Schroeder, Commander of Serbia.

3. Down with Hitler: Volks-Traitor, Volks-Betrayer, Volks-Seducer. [This pamphlet used the Allies' "V" for victory sign.]

4. Who Is Lying?: The Wehrmachtsbericht [German Armed Forces News] Are Untrue.

5. One and a Half Million: German Losses Have Reached One and a Half Million in Russia. Listen to BBC London to hear the truth. [The pamphlet listed the times of scheduled broadcasts.]

6. What They Withhold: Losses in Russia Not Being Reported to the Public.

7. 137th Infantry Division: Heavy Losses Reported in that Division.

8. Where Is Rudolf Hess: The Real Reasons Reported for His Flight to Britain.

9. Only Hitler Is the Guilty One: The Reasons for Reprisal Raids over Germany by the R.A.F.

After printing the small handbills, Helmuth started on some full page dissertations. A total of twenty different subjects were covered over the course of our resistance. To list a few:

1. The Voice Of Conscience: A Christmas Message from Rudolf Hess, Originated in England

2. The Nazi Reichsmarshal: Hermann Goering and the Failure of His Luftwaffe!

3. The Hitler Youth We Are Forced to Join: Exposé of the Leaders of the Hitler Youth.

4. Comrades-in-Arms in the North, South, East, and West: Overview of the Military Status on All Fronts. The Sinking (4X) of the Ark Royal , "Iron Savings," Forced Donations to Finance the War.

5. A Wave of Oil: Gasoline Shortages in Germany

6. Perfidies ROME: German/Italian Axis and Their Problems.

7. Speeches by Hitler: A Salty Critique Thereof.

8. In the East Asiatic Theatre Are Many Bases Left for Attack: Appeal to End the War by Toppling Hitler. Hints About the Mysterious Deaths of Field Marshal von Reichenau, General Udet, and Colonel Moelders.

9. *I Have Calculated Everything:* The Defeat of the German Army Due to the Lack of Winter Clothing and Supplies.

An invitation to the German people to join with the Allies in the Ruetli Oath, which demonstrats the resolve of the Allies to win. The oath goes as follows:

> We want to be a brotherhood united and never part, despite danger or want. We want to be free, as our fathers were. Rather death, than to live in slavery! We put our trust in the almighty God, and are not afraid of the tyranny of men!

10. 1942, the Decisive Year: An Invitation to the German People to Do Away with the Nazi Regime.

11. The Rudolf Hess Mystery: Why the Government's Second in Command Left Germany to Sue for Peace in England.

12. Weekend Incarceration: German Youth Are Being Intimidated through Weekend Incarcerations [see copy at the end of this chapter for full text].

13. *The Voice of the Homeland:* What the Bible Has to Say About Hitler [see text at end of chapter].

To my surprise, not one of these leaflets was turned into the Rothenburgsort service office of the Gestapo. But, other offices in the Hammerbrook area received reports of leaflets being dropped off in the neighborhood.

The party members were disturbed, to say the least, at finding these leaflets in mailboxes and telephone booths, particularly since all the leaflets had an invitation printed on them, "Dieses ist ein Kettenbrief, darum weitergeben" ("This is a chain letter, pass it on").

Helmuth was quite selective in choosing people to involve in his enterprise. Yet, he felt such a great sense of personal urgency that sometimes he threw caution to the wind and allowed his true feelings to show at inappropriate times. One day he told me of the discussions he held at his place of work at the Social Services Department, the Bieberhaus. As he and the other apprentices talked of political developments, Helmuth cautiously shared his contempt for the system. At one point he even gave a talk among the young people, challenging them to be more critical of political conditions. When I learned of this, I grew very concerned about Helmuth's safety and asked him to be more careful. I didn't realize he was planning to expand his resistance movement even further by bringing in an ever larger number of conspirators to help distribute the leaflets. I learned later that he'd even cultivated ties with communistic youth organizations, like the Wieczorek group, which he met in the Bismarck Bathhouse in Altona. At the time, Karl-Heinz and I were closest to him. Arthur Sommerfeld was also involved and knew his plans to some extent. But we were only involved in distributing the leaflets on a local level. It was about this time that Helmuth found a co-conspirator in Gerhard Duever, a young man who worked with him at the Bieberhaus. Together, they struck a plan to translate the BBC news into French so it could be passed on to prisoners of war imprisoned in Germany. He also sent these leaflets to the soldiers on the front lines. They even found a printing shop in Kiel where two willing workers agreed to print the leaflets on a secret night shift, in much greater quantities than Helmuth could produce on the branch's typewriter.

As things heated up, Gerhard passed some leaflets on to two other young men named Kurt and Horst Zumsande in an attempt to get them to translate the messages into French. This was done in the presence of another friend, Karl-Horst Pipo. After looking them over, the young men tried to return the leaflets to Gerhard, but he insisted that they at least read them for their political sentiments.

The problems really began when Gerhard and Helmuth tried to find another translator. As bright as Helmuth was, he wasn't a trained and hardened spy. It was a combination of his innocence and zeal that betrayed him. On 20 January 1942, Helmuth and Gerhard entered the room where Werner Kranz was working and tried to enlist his help in translating the leaflets. When Kranz looked at the text of the leaflets, he immediately refused to help and gave them back. This activity caught the attention of Heinrich Mohns, the office Betriebsobmann (political overseer). He came over and asked what was going on and if it was illegal. At this, Helmuth and Gerhard just picked up the leaflets and left. This intrigued Mohns so much that he confronted Kranz for an explanation. Kranz confessed that the papers were enemy propaganda that Huebener wanted him to translate into French.

The next day Mohns confronted frightened Kranz and Gerhard Duever together, demanding they turn the papers over to him. Not having any experience in these matters and having no support group, Duever, as frightened as a teenage boy would be, said he didn't have any with him but was expecting to get some from Helmuth later on. They both agreed to help in obtaining the leaflets. It took Duever until 4 February to bring two copies of the literature in, having been reminded constantly by Mohns to do so. It was the next day, 5 February 1942 that the Gestapo was notified. They immediately came to the office and arrested Helmuth and Gerhard.

The Gestapo agents took them to their homes to conduct a thorough search for incriminating evidence. This wasn't a problem for Gerhard Duever because he'd been given advance warning and had removed all traces of his activity. He hadn't told Helmuth of what was coming, so they found an abundance of materials at his home. In the typewriter, (the branch had allowed Helmuth to bring it home) they found the last leaflet, still being written, with the title "Who is Harassing Whom?" They also confiscated the Rola Radio and everything else used to prepare the leaflets and took them to Gestapo Headquarters in Hamburg, Stadthausbruecke 8, for the first interrogation.

As for me, I wasn't aware that anything had happened to end our short lived resistance movement. On the following Sunday, Karl-Heinz and I both wondered where Helmuth was. "Maybe he's late," I told Karl-Heinz, but we both had a feeling of foreboding.

At the end of our worship meeting, the branch president announced that he'd like everyone to stay seated after the service for a special meeting. It was there that he dropped the "bomb." Helmuth Huebener, a member of the St. Georg branch, had been arrested a few days before by the Gestapo. He told us that he didn't have any details but knew it was for political reasons. He also said that as his branch clerk, Helmuth had been given use of the meetinghouse typewriter to write to servicemen in the field, but had misused that trust to write his antigovernment propaganda, which had resulted in its confiscation.

I felt like somebody had just kicked me in the stomach. When I looked over at Karl-Heinz, he met my gaze, and I knew he was feeling the same way. I felt like this was the end of the world. I wanted to go crawl into a hole somewhere and hide for the rest of my life. With that announcement began some of the most fearful and tortuous days of my life—days spent waiting to find out if the Gestapo would learn of my involvement in Helmuth's anti-Nazi activity.

Exhibit #1—Sample of the small, $1/4$ page leaflets written by Helmuth Huebener:

ONLY HITLER IS THE GUILTY ONE!

Through the limitless war in the air, several hundred thousand unprotected civilians have been killed.

But the R.A.F. (British Royal Air Force) is not to blame for these killings. Their flights are only in reprisal for the raids of the Luftwaffe over Warsaw and Rotterdam, where unarmed women and children, cripples and old men were killed. (Din A6)

HITLER IS TO BLAME!

Exhibit #2—Samples of the full page dissertations:

Leaflet I.

WEEKEND INCARCERATION

German boys! Do you know the country without freedom, the country of terror and tyranny?

Yes, you know it well, but are afraid to talk about it. They have intimidated you to such an extent that you don't dare talk for fear of reprisals. Yes, you are right; it is Germany—The Hitler-Germany!

Through their unscrupulous terror tactics against young and old, men and women, they have succeeded in making you spineless puppets to do their bidding.

But it's you, German boys, who must also suffer under the Gestapo terror. You are especially mistreated in the H.Y. [Hitler Youth]!

"You are the future of Germany," they tell you. But then you are tyrannized and punished for any little offense.

The "Weekend Karzer" [Weekend Jail] is an affront that tops everything. For the smallest infraction during Hitler Youth duty, you will be sentenced to several days of incarceration. You will have to spend your nights in a small room, with the temperature reaching the boiling point, suffering the indignities of a condemned criminal.

Yes, this is the future of Germany!

Exhibit #3— Leaflet W.

THE VOICE OF THE HOMELAND.

"The Bible is not God's word. Merely a scheme of the Jewish world to enslave mankind. The product of an overactive fantasy."

This is the red thread which is found in each of the "freespiritual" or "neo-heathenistic" filth-pamphlets. "The Bible, Not God's Word." That is the title of one of the filthiest and most intemperate brochures of the great Anti-Christ, General Ludendorffs.

Why all this campaign against the Bible, holy writ? The answer to this question should not be too difficult if one knows the contents of the Bible, especially the many prophecies which pertain mostly to the latter days, to the days when heathenism and idolatry will take the upper hand, when the great Anti-Christ will arise in the midst of a peaceful period and will conquer with power or with cunning one country, one kingdom after another.

This time has come now, the Anti-Christ has established his "Reich." Ludendorff knows this just as Hitler does, and they are attempting to take the Bible away from the German Volk, so that they will not be able to see through the insidious plans of Hitler and his followers in advance.

Christians, arise, open the Bible, read what it says in the Book of the Prophet Daniel, 11:20:

> And in his place shall
> Stand up a vile person, to
> Whom they did not intend to
> Give the honor of the kingdom,
> But he shall come in the midst of peace,
> And obtain the kingdom by flatteries.

To whom does this better apply than to the Fuhrer: by means of bold phrase-mongering and grandiose promises he and his comrades succeeded in winning the majority in the Reichstag.

(Translated by Alan F. Keele for *Sunstone Magazine*, Volume 5, No. 6 — used with permission of Alan F. Keele)

CHAPTER FIVE

THE GESTAPO CLOSES IN

The news of Helmuth's arrest hit Karl-Heinz and me like a thunderbolt out of a clear blue sky. We were speechless—afraid that even by looking at each other someone would point their finger at us and say, "They were always close to young Huebener; they must have been in it together!" The house of cards we had built together was suddenly tumbling down. Our friend and leader was arrested; what would happen to us? The thrill and excitement of our activities was replaced by gnawing terror of what might happen.

After Church, Karl-Heinz and I walked home our separate ways hoping not to attract attention. When my mother got home, she asked me what I knew about it. "Nothing, Mother," I lied, trying not to worry her.

But she gave me a long look, as only a mother can, and said, "We shall see!" I knew she was looking right through me and sensed that I had lied. But, to my relief she dropped the subject and let me return to my household duties. That night I tossed around in bed and worried about what would happen to me. I could see Helmuth facing the Gestapo. I'd heard of the brutal methods they used to interrogate people. I couldn't help but remember what Heinrich Worbs had told us about their cruelty. I prayed fervently to Heavenly Father to help Helmuth, to give him strength to withstand the torture.

My mind returned to the conversations we had held in the happier days when we were plotting our antipropaganda moves. Naturally the subject had come up about what to do if

one of us got caught. We'd each vowed that the captured individual would take all the blame upon himself and not give
the others away.

I now asked the question over and over, "Can Helmuth
withstand the torture?" I prayed over and over that he
could—for my sake. On the other hand, I wanted to stand
next to him and take my share of the punishment, so he
would not have to face it alone. Such was the conflict and turmoil in my mind.

The biggest question facing me now was what to do? Should
I try to sneak out of the country, go underground, or hope it
would all pass without me being implicated? I had heard of
people hiding in other cities. People had escaped to Switzer-
land, Sweden, or even England. For several days I contemplated
leaving the country—to leave everything behind me and run
away. I contacted several sources having connections to neutral
or enemy countries. I had to be careful in contacting them so as
to not arouse suspicion. Informants were everywhere.

One of the journeymen at the Norddeutsche Kohlen &
Koks Werke, my place of work, had an uncle in Sweden. He
was always talking about Sweden and how wonderful it was,
so I thought he might be a good contact to help me find my
way to that neutral country. I read everything I could get hold
of about Sweden—the people, the geography, the life-style,
etc. Then I had a long conversation with the journeyman, who
was more than eager to tell me everything I wanted to know.
Just when I was ready to ask if he could help me get there, the
shop Nazi stepped up and asked why I was asking so many
questions. Apparently he'd picked up bits and pieces of our
conversations. I told him I was trying to write an essay about
Sweden and was gathering information for it. He exhorted me
to "write about Germany, and how great a nation it had become under Hitler who will one day rule the whole world."

"Perhaps that is why I am studying about Sweden," I
replied. "About why they wanted to remain neutral in this
'interesting' scheme of events."

"Hah," he crowed. "Sweden is just a haven for a lot of
Jews and should be overrun. All of Europe should be a German protectorate." At this, the other journeyman got into the
conversation by telling the Nazi to be quiet, that this was a
place of work and not a party meeting. Master Truebe walked

into the shop at this moment and told everyone to break it up and go back to work. And so I watched my chance to pursue this avenue of escape disappear in a moment. Because of the Nazi's prying eyes, I never again found a safe opportunity to ask the journeyman about getting to Sweden.

Soon it was 11 February, my sixteenth birthday. We had a small, but nice birthday party at our home that allowed me a few hours to forget the ominous cloud that hung over my head. My mother had baked several cakes, including the famous Rosinenpuffer (raisin cake) I liked so much. My grandmother, Alma Meyer was there with her son Carl and his wife Lisa. The Meyers were a happy family that liked music. My Uncle Alfred played the violin, Uncle Carl the bass fiddle (as well as several other instruments), and I played the clarinet. We played and sang old German folk songs and laughed with each other. Just before parting, we sang a few Church hymns.

As our guests were leaving, the ominous feeling returned. I felt that such a time as this would never come again. Perhaps I would be a castaway in a foreign land or an inmate of a Gestapo concentration camp. The thought came that I needed to contact the underground for help in leaving the country. But how? I turned to gaze on my mother and felt the warmth and security that comes from a family. I felt I just couldn't leave them. If I did escape, the Gestapo would take out its wrath on these people I loved so much! I had seen whole families sent to camps due to the escape of one offending member.

The days passed slowly, leaving me with the daily inner turmoil, not knowing which way to go or what to do. My heart would miss a beat or two each time I passed policemen on the street. I thought everyone knew of my deeds, and that it was just a matter of time until they pounced on me. On Saturday, 14 February, I thought of contacting Karl-Heinz to find out how he was holding up but cast the thought aside for fear it would raise suspicions even further.

The next day, Sunday, I went to church as usual, looking anxiously for Karl-Heinz. I couldn't find him anywhere. As I went outside to wait for him, his sister Carla and her girl friend, Lucy Erikson, saw me and came toward me. Carla looked around, checking to make sure that nobody was close by, and said, "Karl-Heinz got arrested by the Gestapo last Tuesday—they are going to get you next!" If she'd have hit me over the head with a sledgehammer, it couldn't have stunned me more! "What are you going to do?" she asked.

"I don't know. What can I do?" was my feeble response.

By now it was time to enter the chapel. I walked as though I were in a trance. Some of the members asked if I was feeling well, because I looked so pale, but I didn't answer them. I barely heard the announcement from the branch president that a second member of the branch was arrested during the previous week. Nor did I hear his sermon about the importance of keeping the laws of the land and supporting and sustaining the Fuhrer who was ordained of God, etc. What I did hear were the whispered remarks of some of the members, such as, "Those poor boys. I wonder what made them do it?" and "Who else is behind this?"

Someone else said, "How terrible, getting arrested by the Gestapo—they do awful things to people!" Then there were other voices, full of anger and hurt, such as "How could they oppose a government that is installed of God?" Another asked, "Doesn't this violate the twelfth Article of Faith which says we should be subject to our rulers and sustain the laws of the land?" Someone else spoke up and said, "They surely have broken the law. I hope they throw the book at them!" And finally, "That is treason, and they should be shot—if I had a gun I would shoot them myself!" With that I had heard enough, and I ran out of the meetinghouse, terrified. The last words I heard were, "I think he is one of them!"

I ran all the way home. Normally it would take a full hour to cover the distance from the church, but I made it in just thirty minutes. The strain of the exercise made me feel better, but soon the fear and anxiety returned. I reasoned that if they got Karl-Heinz, they would soon be coming for me. The question was, what should I do? Should I try to escape or stay put and face whatever was in store for me at home? My mind raced to think of ways out. I thought of our tenant, Jan Gorter. He was from Holland, but had been "drafted" to work in Germany. He talked freely about conditions in Holland, and how they hid Jews from the Gestapo in Amsterdam. The occupation of Holland was harsh; the German army held a tight leash on the population. In spite of that, he said, the Dutch underground had smuggled many Jews and other "politicals" to England right under the noses of the Germans.

At this desperate moment I took a chance, and asked him how one could get in touch with the Dutch Underground if one were trying to escape. He gave me a long look and asked if I was in some kind of trouble. I looked away and said, "Oh no, not me." I hated to lie to him because he was such a good friend, but I had to be careful not to reveal myself to anyone. I told him I was asking for a friend who was in trouble with the police, who might want to escape to avoid prosecution. Jan got very serious and told me to stay out of it, that it was very difficult to get to England by going through Holland because many of the local police were friendly toward the Germans. There were also too many "Mussert" followers in Holland who would inform the Gestapo of any strangers there.

Because Jan had joined the Church shortly after moving in with us, he'd been at the meetings and learned of the arrest of Helmuth and Karl-Heinz. I could see he was about to ask me if I was involved as well. Fortunately, I didn't have to answer this kind man (who would one day become my stepfather), because at that moment my mother walked in. She marched straight to me and said, "Rudi, we have to talk!" She told me she had been worrying about me since the day she heard of Helmuth's arrest. She knew Helmuth and I were very close and surmised that I had something to do with his political activities.

She went on to say that she knew I had lied to her but was hoping I would come to her and tell her the truth. After she heard the news that Karl-Heinz had been arrested also, she decided she couldn't wait any longer to talk about it. She concluded her speech by saying she knew for certain that I was involved when she saw me get up and leave the meeting. Now she wanted the whole truth. It was very difficult to confess to her. "I lied to you because I did not want you to be involved or get hurt," I told my mom.

"I have figured that out by myself," she said. "But I was hurt that you didn't feel you could trust me. What are you going to do?"

"What can I do?" I replied. "If I run away, they would get you and put you in a concentration camp. I cannot have that on my conscience."

"Why did you do this thing anyway? Did you not know it was against the law?" she asked.

"Mother, I had to do something. I could not just look on and let the Nazis maim, hurt, and kill all the good people of this country," I replied. "Remember what they did to Heinrich Worbs!"

Then my mother cried out, "They are going to arrest you too, and only God knows what they will do to you!" Then the realization hit me with full force, and we both cried in each other's arms.

That night I heard my mother pray to the Lord, asking him to spare me or somehow let the destroying Nazi force pass me by. In spite of her prayer, I spent another sleepless night in my bed. I worried about my mother and my other loved ones and wondered what might happen to them if I was arrested.

The next Monday and Tuesday went by without incident. Yet, I couldn't shake the gnawing feeling in the bottom of my stomach that something awful was about to happen to me. On Wednesday, 18 February, I went to class at the vocational school at Angerstrasse 7. The morning hours were spent learning about steel fabrication, math, and chemistry. At the beginning of the technical drafting class, there was a knock on the door, and I turned to see the principal enter the classroom. He talked for a few moments to my teacher, then they both came to my desk. "Would you please accompany me to my office?" the principal said. "There are two gentlemen who want to talk with you."

I felt again as if somebody had kicked me in the stomach, for I knew that the two "gentlemen" were from the Gestapo. When we entered the principal's office I saw the two in their leather coats and black wide brimmed hats.

"Are you Rudolf Wobbe?"

"Yes, I am."

"Geheime Staatspolizei, mitkommen!" (Gestapo. Come with us!) The identification of these agents was done by quickly flipping the left lapel of their coat to reveal the badge of the dreaded Gestapo.

"But my things are still in the classroom," I stammered.

"Never mind those, come with us *now!*" they said, grabbing me by the arms. They hurried me outside to a waiting car. I was pushed into the back seat next to Officer Muessener. Kommissar Wangemann drove the car. Not a word was spoken as we traveled.

Soon I noticed they were proceeding toward my home. When we reached our house in Rothenburgsort they escorted me upstairs to our apartment on the second floor. My mother was already waiting for us. There were tears in her eyes. Apparently they went there before getting me from school. First, they searched the main rooms of our apartment, finding nothing. Then they asked Mother where I slept. When she showed them, they really went to work. They searched everywhere, including drawers, corners, chests, and shelves. They even pulled out every book on the bookshelf, flipping furiously through the pages. Then they looked under the bed, but didn't find anything there, either. All this time I stood rigid with anxiety as I watched them come closer and closer to my hiding place. I silently prayed to Heavenly Father to strike them with blindness so they wouldn't find it.

On the wall, next to my bed, hung a tapestry depicting an elk in the rutting season, bellowing a challenge to another bull elk. Behind this tapestry was my secret hiding place. The wallpaper had come loose, creating a small pocket in which I had hidden several of the large leaflets. At last Kommissar Wangemann came up and shook the tapestry and made fun of it by pointing to the bull elk and saying, "You will be bugling like this bull elk before we get through with you!" Both of them had a good laugh at this statement. But my prayers were answered, for they didn't find my secret cache. With that they stopped searching and told me to get ready to leave. It was hard to say good-bye to my mother. Her last words were, "God bless you, my son, I will keep praying for you." Then two Gestapo men took me down the stairs and into the car.

The next stop was the Gestapo headquarters at Stadthausbruecke in the center of Hamburg. I was escorted directly to the interrogation room. I was instructed to stand in the middle of the room while Muessener and Wangemann sat in chairs on each side of me. During the interrogation, I had to constantly turn my head from left to right to answer their rapid fire questions. First they asked my name, where I lived, father's name, mother's name, etc. Then they asked me Hitler's birthday, the name of the Nazi party, how many points in the party program, etc. Fortunately, this was data that had been hammered into our minds daily, while in school. By this time I was getting a little bit dizzy from turning my head all the time. Whenever I tried to answer without looking at them, they barked at me to face them when answering a question. Later, I realized this was one of their methods of irritating a prisoner so that he would lose his concentration.

Now they turned the interrogation to the actual reason for my arrest. They asked me if I ever listened to BBC London or any other foreign broadcast. At this time I remembered the promise we made to protect each other, even to the point of telling lies, if necessary. So, I lied about listening to BBC London in Helmuth's apartment. They didn't like my answer, so Wangemann hit me in the face with his fist. I stumbled over to Muessener, who shoved me back to the center again. "Did you listen to BBC London at Huebener's house?" they asked again, and again. Instead of weakening me, this abuse made me more determined not to give them what they wanted. I began answering them slower and slower. They interpreted my behavior to mean I was slow witted. That was okay by me, because it caused them to slow down a bit. I was scared stiff, but tried to keep a rational head in spite of the terror they inflicted upon me.

Then, they changed tactics. This time they tried to get me to admit that my mother knew all along what I was doing and that she had supported me in this treasonous act. I saw through their ploy and denied their accusations vehemently. I told them I had tried to get the BBC on our radio receiver when I was alone, but that the apparatus was too old and couldn't pick up the BBC. With this they seemed satisfied and dropped the attempt to implicate my mother.

Now they changed their focus to the actual case against us. He said Karl-Heinz had confessed to telling me about the handbills.

"But, he told me that he burned them right away," I told them, trying to shield Karl-Heinz.

"Never mind that; just tell us about yourself," they said. "Huebener told us he gave you twenty handbills with the instruction to distribute them."

"That's a lie," I told them, but I hardly had the words out of my mouth, when I felt the jackboot of Inspector Wangemann against my knee. He kicked me so hard, I fell to the floor. While I was lying there he kicked me some more, this time in my ribs. Wangemann was reaching for the club which hung on the wall when a knock on the door stopped him and saved me from getting a more severe beating.

The door was opened by an SS guard who said, "The transport to KOLAFU is getting ready to leave. Do you want him to be on it?" The guard's question was directed to Wangemann, who took a moment before answering to regain his composure.

"Take him. We will have him back in the morning any-way."

My days filled with the terror of waiting and wondering were over, but my ordeal had just begun.

CHAPTER SIX

PRETRIAL IMPRISONMENT

I was taken downstairs to board the "Gruene Minna" (our term for the prisoners' bus, which meant, "Green Tin Can"). It was to take us to KOLAFU (a contraction of the camp's full-name, Concentration Camp Fuhlsbuettel). I looked around hoping to find a friendly face, but didn't recognize anyone. A few of us had to wear shackles, which I later learned meant that we were considered hard cases. Two guards were posted in the back of the bus to make certain there was no communication between the prisoners. I couldn't see where we were going since the bus had no side windows. Finally, the bus came to a stop, the back door was opened, and we were told to stand up and get out in single file. As we got up, the fellow next to me whispered in my ear, "Watch out for 'der Lange Paul,'" (the Tall Paul). It didn't take long to figure out who he was talking about, because this giant of a man towered some eight inches above all the other guards. He must have been six foot eight inches tall. Not only that, he stood out from the other guards in brutality as well. His Gummiknueppel (hard rubber truncheon) was never idle. Each of us got to feel it on our backs. "Hurry, hurry, march, march," he screamed, driving us on with his stick. If that didn't make you go fast enough, he'd reward you with a swift kick to the rear.

After getting past Paul, we were led upstairs to the cell-block. I was placed in a cell with an older man who, I later found out, had been a member of the dreaded SS. Because of his prewar experience as an accountant, he had been assigned to the treasury department of the SS. As bad luck would have it, he didn't receive his scheduled paycheck in time for his wife's birthday and didn't have money to buy flowers for her. He asked his supervisor if he could loan him five marks for the day or two it would take for the checks to arrive. His supervisor told him he didn't have any money either, but it would be all right to take five marks out of the cash drawer as an advance against his pay. The accountant carefully wrote out a signed IOU and placed it in the drawer in exchange for the money. All seemed in order.

He didn't know that his supervisor was setting a trap for him. After my cellmate had left for the day, the supervisor called an auditor in for a secret audit of the cash account—which showed up as being five marks short. The IOU had conveniently disappeared. When my accountant friend showed up for work the following Monday, he was immediately arrested for theft and malfeasance in office. Needless to say, he was a bitter man, especially after the treatment he received from his fellow officers in the SS. They came up with particularly demeaning duties for him, to show how much they despised him for betraying their fraternity. To his dismay, no one would listen to his side of the story of how he'd been set up by his supervisor.

In a way, I was fortunate to be assigned with him as a companion, because he taught me how to survive in prison. For example, he told me that whenever a guard opened the door I had to jump up, stand at attention against the wall opposite the door and report in a loud voice, "Schutzhaftgefangener (protective custody prisoner) Wobbe reporting!" Protective custody actually meant that the state was protecting itself from you, by reeducating you to become a better and more useful citizen.

The next morning, we were forced to awake at 5:00 A.M. with the order to make our beds and clean the room. My cellmate knew what to expect and told me what to look out for, such as wiping the dust off everything, including the light shades and window sill. Sure enough, when the guard showed up, he checked every corner with a white glove and even stepped on a stool to reach high up on the window in search of some wayward dust. After a long search, he managed to find some neglected grime, which he promptly smeared in the face of the SS prisoner. As the guard inspected the toilet bowl, he called the old man over to take a look. As my cellmate bent over to look, the guard forced his face into the bowl screaming, "You call this clean? Does it smell clean?"

"I am sorry, sir!" replied the SS prisoner.

"Sorry, you say—I should think you'd know better, being a former SS officer!" With this he slapped the prisoner across the face with a set of keys, ripping the skin open so that blood ran freely. With that, the guard left the cell, laughing outside while telling another guard how he had "told this ex-officer off!" Apparently, the guard held a lesser rank in the SS than the inmate.

When it was over, I told my cellmate I was sorry that I might have caused him some trouble through my sloppiness in cleaning the cell. He just shrugged and said this occurred every morning whether I was there or not. This made me feel a little better, but I still could not understand the brutality of the guards to one of their own. Little did I know what they were capable of.

It was time to get ready for the one hour trip to Gestapo headquarters for my next interrogation. As soon as the bus arrived, we marched to a large room called the Spiegelsaal (The Hall of Mirrors). As I entered, I looked around but could find no mirrors, just bare walls. I soon understood the meaning of the name, though. We were all lined up around the outside edges of the room and were forced to stand with our noses against the wall for many hours. Anyone caught moving or turning his head would get a slap in the back of the neck to force his nose against the wall again. Thus, the Hall of Mirrors was a place where prisoners were to reflect on the gravity of their predicament.

After two hours of standing there, people began passing out and crumbling to the floor. They were quickly revived by kicks and beatings from the guards. During this time the names of different prisoners were called out so they could be escorted to their individual interrogation rooms. After two and a half hours, I heard my name called and was soon on my way up the stairs to face my tormenters. They were Kriminal-Sekretaer Muessener and Kommissar Wangemann again.

As I entered the room, I noticed the furniture had been re-arranged and that there were bloodstains on the floor between the two tables. Wangemann was in a raw mood that morning. He slapped his rubber stick against his hand and I noticed it left bloodstains on it. He noticed the stain and walked over to a corner of the room to wipe it on bloody towel. He turned and walked up to me, pushed the stick into my throat, and said, "Now we want to talk with you and we'd better have a good talk or I'll have to soften you up a little!" With that he pushed my head back with the stick so forcefully that I lost my balance and hit my head against the wall behind me.

"Come back here," he yelled. "I am not through with you yet!" He then whacked me in the stomach. "Huebener told us that he gave you about twenty handbills," he started out. "What did you do with them?"

"I passed them out," I answered.

"Where did you pass them out?"

"In the streets of Rothenburgsort," I replied. I was deliberately slow in answering his questions, which really riled him. He drew close to me, grabbed me by the collar of my jacket and shook me violently while shouting obscenities at me. Then he let go with his right hand, still holding me with his left, and hit me in the face with the back of his hand several times, until my lips were bleeding. "Now let's start again," he said. "But now you better sing, loud and clear—What did you do with the handbills?"

I fought back my tears, swallowed hard a couple of times, and replied, "I dropped them into mailboxes in the apartment buildings."

"Where, what streets?" he screamed.

"Billhorner Roehrendamm, Billhorner Muehlenweg, Markmannstrasse, Lindleystrasse, and Kanalstrasse."

"That's better," he said. "But where else did you leave these handbills?"

"I also posted them on the bulletin boards of the party that were installed in the entrance of the apartment buildings."

"How often did you receive handbills from Huebener?"

I replied, "Twice I received handbills from Huebener; first the small ones, which I distributed, and then four or five copies of the larger ones, the dissertations, which I destroyed after reading them."

"Do you know of any other people that have received leaflets from Huebener?" he asked.

"No, I have no knowledge of any others," I lied, still trying to shield the others.

The line of questioning changed to the radio broadcasts. "How many times have you listened to the BBC London radio newscasts in Huebener's apartment?" he asked.

"As I have stated before, I have not listened to any radio broadcasts in Huebener's apartment. I only visited him there a couple of times, because we were friends. On one of those visits, after his grandparents had gone to bed, he gave me some handbills." My only hope was that they would believe my lies so they would not push me to incriminate my friends. Even though my mother had always taught me to tell the truth no matter what the circumstances, I rationalized that in this case I would have to lie.

Wangemann now sat down and Muessener took over the interrogation. They played their roles very well. Wangemann was the tough and brutal one while Muessener was more subdued and supportive.

Muessener asked me, "Why did you do this, boy? Were you dissatisfied about something or angry at anybody?"

"No, I had no reason," I lied. In truth I had plenty to talk about, but this clearly wasn't the place or person to tell. I was learning very fast. "I don't know why I did this," I went on. "I later realized that my actions were very stupid." I thought that was what they wanted to hear from me. I also noted that Muessener was taking notes all the time Wangemann was interrogating me.

Apparently this last answer satisfied them, or perhaps they had other business. To my great relief they called my interrogation off for the day. I was escorted back to the Hall of Mirrors, for another "standing in," which lasted another hour before we were returned to KOLAFU.

As we entered the transport, I noticed one of the station SS guards gave our driver a list of names in addition to the regular check-off list. I didn't think anything of it at the time, but when I saw the same list in the hands of der Lange Paul at the next morning's roll call I became suspicious—especially after he started to read the names from that list. Each of the prisoners called were told to stand two steps in front of the group. When it was my turn he asked me how old I was. I quickly replied that I was sixteen.

"And what are you in here for?" he asked.

"I don't know," I replied. He immediately hit me over the head with his rubber truncheon.

I picked myself up off the ground, understanding that I had given him the wrong answer.

"What are you in here for?" he asked again.

"For passing out handbills," I replied.

"And what was on them?" he asked sarcastically. "A Persil advertisement?" (Persil is a product brand name in Germany, like Tide detergent)

"'Hitler the Murderer' was written on it," I told him.

"You Swine!" he exploded, "I'll teach you not to defile the Fuhrer in my presence!" He then started hitting me again and again, screaming, "You wait, I'll teach you the right way yet!" With that he pushed me back into the line. That was how the day started at KOLAFU, before we even got to Gestapo Headquarters.

Once there, we were reintroduced to the Hall of Mirrors. I tried in vain to locate Helmuth or Karl-Heinz but recalled that I had not seen them on the Gruene Minna on the way into town. Just then I heard my name called out by the SS guard sitting at the table with the telephone on it. I turned around and said, "Here," and another SS man told me to follow him upstairs. I wound up in the same interrogation room again. The scenery had not changed and, much to my dismay, neither had my Gestapo interrogators, Wangemann and Muessener. Today, however, they started out with a different form of interrogation. Muessener sat down behind a desk with a note pad in front of him, while Wangemann stood in the middle of the room with his rubber truncheon in one hand, which he was slapping against his black jackboot. I had to stand in the center of the room at full attention. Wangemann started circling like a vulture does carrion, firing off questions in rapid succession.

"Who is the man, or men, behind this conspiracy?" "What other groups are you affiliated with?" "Who has been paying you to do this?"

At each of my answers he hit me across the back with his truncheon and screamed, "That is a lie. You better tell me the truth!"

"But I am telling you the truth," I pleaded. "What else can I tell you?"

"Let's start from the top again," Wangemann said. "And this time we want the full truth." With that he placed himself in front of me with the rubber truncheon in one hand, slapping it in a steady rhythm in the other hand. He started with, "Who are the men behind this conspiracy? We know that you are too young to have dreamed up something like this."

"Nobody is behind this," I responded. "It is of our own making, and if there should be somebody behind it, I have no knowledge of it, and that is the truth!" Wangemann now placed the truncheon on my chest and pushed me backwards.

"What is the name of the other group you are affiliated with?" he pressed. He didn't like it when I again told him there was no other group and started beating me on the shoulders and back so hard that it forced me to my knees.

Muessener's voice seemed very far away when he quietly said, "You better tell him the truth or he will break every bone in your body."

"But I am telling the truth," I cried. "There is nobody else!" I had my hands wrapped around my head to shield off any more hits. I was sobbing like a baby. "There really is nobody else behind us," I said. "Helmuth wrote the news down in shorthand and later typed it into handbills, and we passed them out afterwards."

Wangemann walked over to the desk where Muessener was sitting, and they talked quietly with each other for a moment. As they exchanged places, I expected more beatings and ducked my head as Muessener approached. Instead, I felt his hand helping me to stand up again.

"Now, let's talk," he said in an almost fatherly fashion, all the while patting me on the back to calm me down. "What can you tell me about the grandparents of Helmuth Huebener—did they listen to the radio, like BBC London?"

"As I have stated before, I have never listened to BBC London news broadcasts in Helmuth's apartment, so I do not know if his grandparents ever listen to any foreign broadcast. I do know that they like to go to bed early, and Helmuth said the BBC Broadcasts started at 10:00 P.M., so I assume they were already sound asleep."

The next statement took me by surprise as my interrogator said, "Your mother knew of your activity, and also listened to the broadcast in your home, didn't she?"

I vehemently denied it, knowing that they were trying to trick me.

"How many other people have you talked to about these handbills?" he asked matter-of-factly. "What about your uncles, Carl and Alfred Meyer? Perhaps you also discussed them with some of the people at your church?"

After Wangemann, the tough and brutal one, it was so tempting to open up to the kind, fatherly Muessener. But I saw that he was simply trying to implicate other people, so I denied ever talking to anyone else. In spite of my denials, he wouldn't let up.

"When you lived at your previous address, Hardenstrasse 29, there were several reactionary elements who also lived in that terrace, such as Heinrich Koch the Communist, August Binder the Social Democrat, and Tedje Behrmann, another Communist. It's true, isn't it, that they supplied you boys with red flags bearing the hammer and sickle, and that you used to play with them, didn't you?"

"Yes, that's true, but I was six years old at the time, and Hitler hadn't even taken over," I replied, somewhat bewildered. He asked if I'd tried to contact these people again, since the start of the conspiracy. "How could I? We moved away from there, and the last report from the old neighborhood was that Koch and Behrmann had been arrested and placed in a concentration camp," I responded.

"Who told you they were in a concentration camp? Tell me their names!"

"I don't know," I told him. "Everybody just knew it." I didn't see myself as noble boy, but I didn't want to be the cause of anyone else receiving the same treatment I was receiving.

They finally let up with the interrogation and called the guard to escort me downstairs to the Hall of Mirrors. I trembled as I stood looking at the wall and tears streamed down my cheeks. Next to me stood an older prisoner who sensed my predicament. He whispered very quietly, "Be calm. Don't let them rattle you—take a deep breath and relax."

Hans (as I later learned his name) then told me, "Remember what you have told them; burn it into your memory, because they will ask you the same questions again and again, so don't deviate from your original statements."

The guard heard the whispering and marched back and forth along the length of the room a few times, trying to spot the perpetrator. After he gave up and returned to the desk, Hans whispered, "Be strong, don't let them get you down—remember, you have to survive!"

That night, when we arrived at the main gate of the prison camp, I saw that Lange Paul already waiting for us in a sour mood again. "Get out, hurry up, you are late again," he shouted, all the time swinging his truncheon at prisoners, who were trying to duck the strikes or shield their heads with their arms. When he saw me, he recognized me from our encounter earlier that morning.

"Well, here is our young conspirator who likes to pass out handbills with lies printed on them about the Fuhrer! I will teach you a thing or two today." With that he started beating me. His strikes came so fast and the pain was so great that I thought that this couldn't be happening—that it was a nightmare from which I would awaken. I fell to the ground and he began kicking me viciously. My will to protect myself, to survive, left me , and I gave myself up to being kicked to death.

Suddenly I felt two strong arms picking me up from the ground, and I was pushed against the wall of the doorway while someone shielded me from Lange Paul's attack with his own body.

I heard a voice whisper, "Just hide yourself behind me, become part of the wall!"

I recognized the voice of my protector as Hans, my friend from earlier in the day. Later I tried to thank him, but didn't have the energy to speak and in the press of prisoners we were soon separated.

I looked for him the following day so I could thank him properly but never saw him again. I never did learn his last name and was left to wonder who this guardian angel was, who was there when I needed him most.

The next morning brought another trip to Gestapo Headquarters, where they went over the same things again and again. I was weak from my beating the night before and my voice shook. This didn't concern them in the least. I remembered the advice of my friend Hans and stuck to the story I had given them the day before. To my surprise, Wangemann and Muessener did not make any fuss, or give me a particularly bad time. They apparently believed my statements. I was glad for this because I feared that under any more beatings, I would have broken down completely and said anything they wanted me to say.

At the end of the interview they gave me a sheet of type-written paper and told me to read it. It was what we had talked about over the course of the interrogation. Muessener asked if that was the way I remembered telling them. I agreed with the report, and they asked me to sign it. I had to write, "I have read this myself and found it a correct statement. Rudolf Wobbe."

After this I was led outside for the guard to take me back to the Hall of Mirrors. I looked around to locate Hans but couldn't find him. Neither did I see Karl-Heinz or Helmuth.

On the trip back to KOLAFU, I was apprehensive about meeting up with the guards again. To my relief Paul wasn't there to greet me. We were shuffled into our cells and that was the end of that day. I was relieved that the severe beatings had apparently ended, but still I did not sleep well that night. I felt such homesickness and loneliness.

The following morning went by without a call to the transport bus. The next day was the same, although we were given time to walk around the yard to stretch our legs. What a sight. Since all the cells were located on the second floor, the guards would open the doors and herd us downstairs like a flock of geese. We then had to march single file in an almost continuous line around the courtyard. Talking or whispering was strictly forbidden. After twenty minutes of this we were herded back to our cells, which we found in a state of disarray. The guards used the so-called free time to search the cells for contraband or other things we were not allowed to have.

On the ninth day after my arrest, 27 February, we were called out for another transport. This time we went to the Untersuchungsgefaengnis Stadt Hamburg (Investigation Prison) in the heart of Hamburg. We were led upstairs past the cells of the death-row candidates. The peepholes in the doors were open and I tried to take a look through one. A guard behind me kicked me so hard that I lost consciousness. Another prisoner picked me up and carried me to the infirmary where we were heading anyway for our medical examination. When I awoke I saw Karl-Heinz standing by my side. Karl-Heinz was complaining to the doctor about my harsh treatment but was told that I was just pretending to be hurt and that he could not waste any time on a faker. When Karl-Heinz protested, he was told to shut up and get back in line.

I was brought to Station #5, Cell #54. The cell had three beds, one wash basin, and one toilet. There was also a table and three stools. The window was facing north and looked out at the park-promenade called the Stadtgraben. By standing on a stool, I was able to look out on that beautiful sight. One had to be careful a guard wasn't watching.

For the first few days I had just one cellmate. On the third day another prisoner was assigned to our cell. His name was Bernhard Rubinke and he was just two years older than I. In spite of his young age, he seemed to be experienced with prison life. I found out later that he had been in and out of corrective institutions all his life. He was a likeable fellow and seemed to go out of his way to befriend me. He showed me what to do and what not to do to get along with the guards. He would stand in front of the spyglass in the door so I could look out the window without being seen by the guard. I didn't know that he was a Gestapo spy who had been placed in the cell with the charge to gain my confidence and trick me into revealing additional information. Before long he had me talking about my case and my feelings in general. When I asked him about his case he became evasive and said he was there for stealing, fraud, and forgery. I wanted him to be more specific, but he said his case was still pending and he could tell me no more. The other fellow in our cell had been caught robbing a store. We learned all this in conversations that took place over the course of several weeks. It was great to be free of any further interrogations during this period.

In May I was called to be a witness in another case. A fellow from my trade school had sold me 2,000 grams of food stamps because he needed money. It turns out he'd stolen them. When questioned, he revealed that I had received some of the stamps. When the judge found out I was being held on political charges already, he dismissed me and forwarded the charges to the Gestapo.

On 28 May I received the indictment papers from the Volksgerichtshof (the People's Court) in Berlin with the trial date 11 August 1942. The charge was Preparation to High

Treason and Aiding & Abetting the Enemy. The indictment papers were sealed and stamped on top "TOP SECRET." Because of the Top Secret designation assigned our case, the guard told me I could have a private cell if I wanted one. I declined the invitation. In retrospect, this was a mistake, because while there, the spy, Rubinke, was able to get me to divulge some of the details in the indictment papers that I was supposed to keep secret. In fact, he constantly probed to get me to tell him information that could be used to incriminate me.

One day he asked how it was in KOLAFU and if I met any SS guards there. This question should have made me suspicious since I'd never told him I'd been at KOLAFU before coming to the Investigative Prison. But, I was naive and trusting, and let it pass.

"They must have treated you all right there?" he asked.

"They are a bunch of maniacs," I said. "They beat the prisoners for no reason at all." I went on to say that no decent man would ever join the SS and that anybody who volunteered to join the SS might as well commit suicide, because by joining he gave up any right to be called a human being.

He asked what the BBC London was telling the people in their broadcasts. I told him they were telling their listeners about the retreats of the German army in Russia and the high casualty rates of the German troops there. I also told him the people in Holland were having hunger revolts and that the future of the German soldier in Holland looked pretty bleak because of the opposition. I knew this first hand, I said, because we have a Hollander living with us. I went on to say that the occupation of Holland, Denmark, and Norway had nothing to do with normal warfare, but was a simple case of murder and plunder. I was really riled up and said much more than I should have.

On 10 July 1942, I was suddenly called to appear at the Gestapo headquarters again. It was there I found out why Rubinke had been asking so many questions. Not that anyone told me he was put in the cell for that reason, but I could figure it out by the questions the interrogators were asking. As I listened to their questions, I realized that Rubinke not only divulged all I had told him but also must have added his own comments to make me look even worse. Muessener asked again if Helmuth's grandparents had listened in to the BBC broadcasts. I told him that I didn't believe they ever had. He also alluded to the fact that Helmuth must have had an agent who gave him money for the printing of the handbills. Rubinke even held that I'd participated in a burglary. I denied all these things and then asked Muessener what was wrong with Rubinke that would cause him to accuse me of such things. Somehow I had the feeling that Muessener believed me, because he did not press the issues that Rubinke had reported to them. When I asked how he could believe a man like Rubinke, who had spent most of his life in reform schools and corrective institutions for fraud, forgery, and stealing, he only said, "I know his background, but we have to investigate his report."

When I came back to my cell, Rubinke had been transferred. I don't know what I would have done to him, but I was very angry—at myself for being stupid enough to trust a man like this, and at him for being such a lowlife that he would betray my trust. Of course he did it to receive a reduced sentence. In spite of his questionable credibility, I later learned that the Volksgerichtshof in Berlin thought that Rubinke's testimony was important enough for my conviction that they included him as a witness at the trial.

The days passed slowly for a frightened, confused sixteen-year-old. The cruelty which I'd seen the government turn against so many people in the past was now directed at me and my friends. We were just teenagers who had tried to express a point of view. But that point of view terrorized the Nazis so badly that they saw fit to brutalize and imprison us. So serious did they take our dissenting opinion that soon my friends and I would stand before the highest court in the land, the dreaded Blood Tribunal.

CHAPTER SEVEN

ON TRIAL BEFORE THE BLOOD TRIBUNAL

It was now the summer of 1942. The German army in Russia began to thaw out after a freezing winter and to regroup after being stopped by a tenacious foe that had demoralized even the most patriotic Nazi soldier. In North Africa, the famous Afrika Korps had reached the end of its supply tether just as the British and Americans were reaching full strength. In short, the military situation wasn't going well. A year earlier, Germany had seemed invincible. Now, we were bogged down on every front.

At home, things weren't much better. The nightly bombing raids by the British Royal Air Force started to take a toll. The morale of the German workers fell to new lows as they spent exhausting, sleepless nights in air raid shelters only to come out the next morning to find their homes destroyed. They learned that even the government-built bunkers weren't totally secure. A direct hit by one of Britain's block-buster bombs could wipe out the population of an entire street in one strike. In such an atmosphere it was difficult to maintain the will to go on. The propaganda films of victorious soldiers fighting on foreign soil made the battle-front look like a vacation compared to life on the home front. A lot of people began to question the Nazi propaganda and to doubt what they were being told in the news. In spite of the terror of the Nazi rule, people murmured as they became disillusioned with the Third Reich. The Nazis labeled such attitudes as "defeatism," and put several people on trial for it, but that just made things worse.

Such was the atmosphere as we began our trial for Preparation to High Treason. The government was desperate to regain control of the people's loyalty and to suppress anything that looked like dissent or criticism. We had picked a great time to begin our antigovernment campaign.

It was in the first week of August when I was called out of my cell to be transported to the Volksgerichtshof in Berlin for my trial. I was joined on this excursion by Helmuth, Karl-Heinz, and Gerhard Duever. It was good to see my friends again, but there was little rejoicing due to the awful circumstances that surrounded us.

We went to the railroad station at Altona in one of our famous green prison buses. Before boarding the train, we were handcuffed and chained to the four policemen who were to escort us to Berlin. They placed us in a separate compartment on the express train marked "Police Transport—Entry Forbidden!" Once inside, the guards took off the handcuffs but warned us not to do anything foolish. The police officers were surprisingly friendly and allowed us to talk with each other about anything but our upcoming trial. In spite of this freedom, the ominous approach of our trial proved an obstacle to pleasant conversation. One of the officers tried to cheer us up by saying that if it was up to him he'd give us each a good thrashing, and then send us to the front to fight for our country. What a merciful judge he would have been compared to the one waiting for us in Berlin.

The four-hour journey to Berlin ended with a ride on a World War I vintage bus. At the prison, while awaiting room assignments, I heard a guard in another room call the name "Rubinke." My heart raced, and I strained to hear what would follow. Sure enough, I heard my old cellmate call out an answer. I then heard the watch commander instruct the guard to hold him until the eleventh of August to be a witness in the trial against Huebener, et al. He went on to say that under no circumstances should Rubinke be on the same floor as prisoner Wobbe. At this my heart sank to the floor. Here was another great strike against me. I felt doomed. How foolish I'd been to open up to this false friend. Now I'd have to pay for being so naive.

I was assigned a cell on the third floor. Once a day I was permitted to join the other prisoners in the prison yard for twenty minutes of single-file marching. This was our exercise period. I dreaded this exercise period because I had grown so weak. In the six months in prison, I dropped from 160 pounds to a skinny 102. It became a real effort to climb the three flights of stairs to my cell. The more I stumbled, the more one guard abused me. He'd attack with words like antisocial, reactionary, scoundrel, communist, and, the worst, verraeter (traitor). He always took pleasure in assuring us that we'd soon be hanging by our necks.

On one occasion, after opening the heavy door, he shoved me into the cell so hard that I stumbled against the upturned wall bed. This caused the bed to fall open on the floor. It took all of the strength in my 102 pound frame to set it back up.

I can't say that they didn't feed us. Each day we received three full meals. In the morning we were given 100 grams of bread with some unidentifiable beverage called malt coffee. At noon we were treated to some kind of watery soup. If a cabbage leaf happened to swim in it, it was cabbage soup; if there were a few kernels of barley and a few strands of beef, it was beef barley soup. The main ingredient was always water. The Berlin specialty was beet soup with herring—an awful combination. Whenever the flap in the door was opened by the guard, he called out, "Here, you swine. Eat your swill." At night we were given another piece of bread (sometimes with a dab of margarine as a special treat) and some more malt coffee to wash down our feast.

Three or four days after arriving in Berlin, I was introduced to Dr. Karl Krause, my NSRB-assigned defense lawyer (NSRB stands for National Socialistic Justice Association, a pool of lawyers that actively supported the Nazi party). Having a lawyer at first gave me hope, but his aloof and distant attitude soon told me he wasn't really interested in my case. His first question was whether or not there was anything I wanted to tell him that wasn't in the indictment papers. Instead of a defense lawyer he seemed to be just another form of SS agent conducting an interrogation. I told him very little. When I asked him what he knew about Rubinke, his reply was very evasive. He'd only tell me that Rubinke would be a witness at the trial. This was the extent of our interview which, by the way, was our only pretrial interview.

Tuesday, 11 August 1942—the day set for our trial. At seven o'clock in the morning, we were called out of the cells to report downstairs for transport to the Volksgerichtshof (People's Court) at Bellevuestrasse #15. Shortly before 8:00 A.M. we entered the Courtroom of The Second Senate, to stand before the dreaded Blood Tribunal of Germany—a court created by the Nazis, without constitutional authority, to be the highest court in the land.

The courtroom was staggering in its grandeur and glory. Everything about it spoke of power and majesty of the state. The room featured varying platforms and levels to separate the different players by rank and importance. We were seated to the left of the Judge's Bench with our defense attorneys sitting in front of us on an elevated platform. Across the hall was the Rostrum of the Chief Prosecutor.

What impressed me most was the oversize Emblem of the Golden Eagle, called the Hoheitsadler, perched fiercely upon the Swastika. Some people derogatorily called it the Pleitegeier—the vulture of impending doom and disaster. This giant display filled the wall behind the judges. All too soon the huge doors in the back of the court room swung open and the justices of the Blood Tribunal started to file in. I understood in an instant why they were called the Blood Tribunal. Each justice was dressed in a brilliant crimson robe, the color of blood. On the left breast of each gown was a magnificently embroidered Golden Eagle like the one at the front of the court. They also wore a blood-red cap. I can't describe the feeling of horror this spectacle brought upon me. My life was in the hands of these powerful men—men who did not know the love of God.

There were only a few spectators scattered around the court, but the press turned out en masse. They were servants to the Nazi party which was determined to make this trial an example to other citizens who might get foolish notions.

As I glanced around the room, I spotted Johann Schnibbe, Karl-Heinz's father, who had come from Hamburg to support his son. I also recognized Kriminalsekretaer Muessener from the Hamburg Gestapo office. There were also other witnesses who were there because they knew Helmuth and Gerhard Duever. One was Werner Kranz, who was later chastised by the court for not reporting Helmuth. Another, Horst Zumsande, was a friend of Gerhard Duever who had been called from his army assignment in Thorn. Then there was Heinrich Mohns, the informer at the Sozialverwaltung, Helmuth's place of work. He was the party agent who was responsible for reporting anything suspicious that happened at work, such as Helmuth and Gerhard's whispered conversations. There was also a district magistrate in charge of personnel from the Social Services Department. And finally, the Reichsjugendamt Fuehrung (Youth Leadership Office) sent their director of Judicial Affairs, Officer Hehs.

At the front of the court, wearing the crimson robes, were the justices: The vice president of the People's Court, Engert; Chief Justice Fikeis; and the Attorney General, Dr. Drullmann. Other officers of the court were dressed in the dreaded SA and SS uniforms. They included Brigadier General Heinsius of the motorized SA, Colonel Bodinus from the SS, and Superior District Court President Hartman. A Justice Department Officer in charge of documentation, named Woehlke, was the other official representative. There were enough dignitaries to impress even the most hardened offenders, let alone four teenage boys.

After the court was called to order, in "the name of the German people," the proceedings began. Vice-president Engert read the charges against us—Preparation to High Treason and Aiding and Abetting the Enemy in Times of War. The trial had begun.

I don't really know what I expected the trial to be like, because I'd never been involved in the judicial system. Like my family, I'd always tried to be an honest and dependable citizen who had no reason to clash with the police. I suppose I accepted the textbook version of how things were supposed to be—an impartial judge, an interested and active defense lawyer, a prosecutor who was only interested in justice, and an open press that would report the truth to the people. We were about to learn reality.

The first order of business was to summon the four witnesses to the front of the court where they were warned to maintain secrecy about court proceedings and the importance of honoring their oath to tell the truth. With this, they were excused from the court room to await a summons.

The prosecutor suggested that due to the nature of the trial, the public should be excluded from the proceedings to secure the confidentiality and safety of the country. The Senate approved this application and directed all spectators, including the press, to leave the room immediately. Assured of privacy, the court could proceed as it wanted, without fear of public disclosure or inspection. The spectators weren't excused so that the country might be protected from us, but that the court might be protected from the country.

We lined up in front of the bench to answer several questions from the President of the Court. The questions were standard party type questions, such as the birth date of the Fuhrer (20 April 1889), how many points in the party program (twenty-five), and so on. These are the things we'd learned throughout our school life during political indoctrination sessions. He took time to have the court read a dissertation Helmuth had written as a fifteen-year-old, entitled, "The Plutocrats." Because it was a school assignment, Helmuth had written it in support of the government's program. Of course he had received an "A+" for its brilliance. The Chief Justice was so impressed he declared that if an aspiring young prosecutor had turned in such an article in law school, he would have received all honors for the work. Helmuth had done it as a boy in middle school.

After passing this political I.Q. test, we were asked what we had against the Fuhrer—a man who had freed Germany from foreign oppression, made her great among the nations of the world, and who had brought back a sense of national pride to all her citizens. Indeed, he asked, what could we hold against the man who was at this very moment leading the armed forces into a glorious victory against the Allies? This political tirade went on for several minutes. As the justice warmed to the subject he became angry and started shouting at us, "You snot-nosed kids, what do you know of what is going on in the world today?" He caught himself, and tried to become objective again. (He didn't become more objective, just quieter.) He told us to sit down and then continued his questioning.

At one point, a judge asked us why we made special efforts to distribute the handbills in the workers' section of Hamburg. Helmuth answered the question, "Hamburg will always be reactionary and opposed to the Nazis."

"Not true, you impertinent boy," screamed the Chief Justice.

They started to go through each handbill and dissertation the Gestapo had collected. The president questioned Helmuth at length, recognizing him as the leader of the group. I could not help but admire the way Helmuth handled himself before the court. Here he was, a mere boy, standing before the highest court in the land. Yet, his confidence grew with every passing moment. He answered each question with a clear voice and acted as a man who was very sure of himself. When he was asked if he believed the enemy propaganda more than the German Wehrmachtsbericht (Armed Forces News), he answered without hesitation, "Yes, I do!"

Pressed by the chairman to commit himself even more, Helmuth went on, "Do you actually believe that Germany can win this war?" With that, the judge lost his composure and screamed at Helmuth, "Silence! How dare you speak that way in my courtroom."

As these interchanges went on, I began to get the distinct impression that Helmuth was purposely drawing attention to himself. Not to be in the limelight, but to focus the court's attention on him and away from us. I think he sensed that this would be his last battle, and he was willing to sacrifice himself to protect us. In spite of my fear, I thrilled to see him in action and felt great pride that he was my friend. It seems impossible, but here was a teenager winning a debate with learned lawyers and justices. If ever a man had a finest hour, this was Helmuth's. What a great man he was. What a great friend.

While the judge was passing the leaflets around to the other associates on the bench, I couldn't help but notice their smiles and snickers as they read Helmuth's doggerel verses, especially the one about Reichsmarshal Hermann Goehring, entitled, "Hermann, the fat dude." That one amused everyone so much the president had to call them back to order to regain control. After reading the pamphlets, they questioned the witnesses one by one. When Heinrich Mohns came up, I couldn't help but dislike him. It takes a slimy, spineless individual to inform and betray a fellow worker. Heinrich practically kissed the boots of the party officials in an attempt to endear himself more fully. His performance and testimony made me sick.

To my great surprise and relief, they never called Bernhard Rubinke as a witness. I found out later he had been transferred back to Hamburg the day before the trial because of some foul-up in his registration. As it was, the judge only questioned me about some of Rubinke's statements, which I was able to explain to his satisfaction. Apparently he had enough material on me without Rubinke's testimony. After hearing the witnesses and questioning each of us, the court concluded the admission of evidence against us.

Now it was time for the prosecutor to suggest appropriate sentences for our alleged crimes. This task he turned to with a vengeance. With all the fervor he could muster, he painted us as the most black-hearted villains of the century, worthy of severe punishment.

— Helmuth Huebener: The death penalty, along with dispossession and deprivation of all civil rights for the rest of his natural life. Additionally, confiscation of the radio receiver and typewriter used in the perpetration of the crime.
— Rudolf Wobbe: Seven years imprisonment.
— Karl-Heinz Schnibbe and Gerhard Duever: An undetermined prison term with a minimum time of two years.

Next, our defense attorneys were given the chance to plead in our behalf:

— Dr. Knie, for Huebener, asked for a mild judgment and possible psychiatric examination.
— Dr. Krause, for Wobbe, pleaded for leniency due to the fact that he was only fifteen years of age at the perpetration of the crime. Suggested not more than two years imprisonment.
— Dr. Kunz, for Schnibbe, asked for a lenient judgment with credit given for the time served in the investigative prison before the trial.
— Attorney Kubath, for Duever, pleaded for leniency.

The performance of our attorneys was a sham. They didn't attempt to mount any defense, or offer any legal rebuttal. Rather, they just showed up for the trial knowing we would be found guilty.

The folly of the whole proceeding was demonstrated to me by the fact that after hearing closing arguments, the justices didn't even leave the room to deliberate. They just stuck their heads together for a few moments on the bench, and then announced that they were ready for sentencing. They told the bailiff to open the doors to let the public back in. After things settled down, they gave us the grim news:

— Helmuth Huebener, for listening to a foreign broadcast station and distributing such news through handbills in connection with Preparation to High Treason and Aiding and Abetting the Enemy: *Sentenced to Death and the Deprivation of his Civil Rights and Honors for the Rest of His Life*.

— Rudolf Wobbe, for listening to a foreign broadcast station and distributing this news through handbills in connection with Preparation to High Treason: *Ten Years Imprisonment*.

— Karl-Heinz Schnibbe, for listening to a foreign broadcast station and distributing the same news: *Five Years Imprisonment*.

— Gerhard Duever, for distributing foreign broadcast news: *Four Years Imprisonment*.

— For Wobbe, Schnibbe, and Duever, the five months previously served to be subtracted from the sentences. Radio and typewriter to be confiscated.

The court gave us harsher sentences than those recommended by the prosecutor. Rather than try to reform their wayward youth, mighty Germany chose to destroy us. The judge asked us if we had anything to say, but we were all too shocked to reply—except for Helmuth. He looked up at them with resolve in his eyes and said, "You have sentenced me to die for telling the truth. My time is now—but your time will come!" Fikeis flew into a rage at this and ranted like a madman. I was too numb from shock to actually hear what he said.

One of the judges read the reasons for the judgment rendered. I was too absorbed in trying to contemplate what had happened to concentrate on what he was saying. At a later date, I was able to study the reasoning of the court, and their actions became clear. In five lengthy paragraphs, they tried to explain to the public what could happen in the minds of four young men that would bring them to fight the mighty Nazi empire. They used this reasoning to justify an unjust sentence. First, they argued that Helmuth had to be classified as an adult, because of his above average intelligence and his early matured intellect. Since he was an adult, he had to be treated as a hard-core criminal due to the seriousness of his offense. The crime of distributing foreign propaganda was bad enough, but it was made worse by being distributed in an area that was especially hard hit by the air raids, thus making the population vulnerable to the demoralizing effects of enemy propaganda. Above all, as agent Muessener from the Hamburg Gestapo office stated, many in the working class neighborhoods we visited still held reactionary or Marxist views.

The court went on to say that there really was no choice between a life in prison or the death penalty for Huebener. The protection of the citizenry of Germany demanded his execution. As the accused stated in his essay, "The Plutocrats," "The common good is more important than the rights of the individual." The court considered it especially vindictive of Huebener to turn against the Fuhrer and his country when Germany was surrounded by enemies and fighting for its very survival.

The same conclusions applied to me. The Senate decided that the seriousness of the distribution of foreign news was to be considered especially treasonous for the same reasons as applied in Huebener's case. But, because I had not written the material, the court decided against the death penalty in favor of imposing the maximum prison term of ten years. The reasoning went on that even though I was a juvenile, the circumstances of the war made it impossible for the law to waver from imposing the harshest possible punishment for the crime of opposing the German way of life and endangering the Fuhrer and the country.

The court explained that in finding the remaining two defendants, Karl-Heinz and Gerhard, guilty of listening to foreign broadcasts, it had to impose the penalties attached to that law. Schnibbe's knowledge, through an extended period of time, of Huebener's access to foreign reports and subsequent failure to report him, while seeking more information himself, was inexcusable. Duever also showed an interest in helping Huebener's cause and so was also guilty. They explained that even though these two had far less involvement than Huebener and Wobbe, their willingness to participate made them subject to stern penalties. Hence their five- and four-year sentences.

It was all over by five o'clock. For our acts of conscience, the court had dealt the harshest possible punishment. We were handcuffed and taken to a holding cell in the basement. While passing through the hallway, I noticed people lining our path on both sides. When we passed by they removed their hats and bowed their heads. I heard one say, "Have courage." Perhaps it was just curiosity that made them stand there, but I felt it was an offering of silent support.

I found myself locked in a room with Helmuth and a Swiss spy, who was also sentenced to death. We didn't speak very much. About all we could do was sit on the benches and try to comprehend the proceedings of the day.

Finally, the Swiss spy broke the silence by cursing the Nazis and their methods. He looked at Helmuth and said, "You should not worry, boy; they will probably commute your sentence anyway. But, for me there is no hope. I am thirty-six years old and know better than to hope for a reprieve."

I quickly agreed with him, but Helmuth looked around the cell and pointed to the walls. "Read the inscriptions," he said. "They tell a different story."

I looked around and saw the pathetic scratching of former prisoners who had left a macabre witness of their passing. These notes, left by condemned men, said it all, "God, help Germany in its darkest hour—sentenced to death," followed by a name and a date. Another said, "Marie, take care of the children. I will love you forever." One had a name with an arrow pointing down, meaning death, and the inscription, "Mother, I am too young to die!" The last one, which hit me the hardest, simply said, "God, help us all!"

"Do you still think they don't mean it, Rudi?" Helmuth asked me. "They are all mad with power," he said. Just then we heard the keys rattle in the lock of the door. When it opened, the guard called my name and said, "You are in the wrong cell. These men have to go to Ploetzensee; you go back to Hamburg." As I stood, Helmuth and I embraced for the last time and he said to me, "Rudi, live well, and remember me!" As the tears welled up in my eyes, all I could say was, "Helmuth!"

I was escorted to another cell to join the others. I was handed a piece of bread, which I ate while still sobbing. After a short time we were herded into a prison bus for transport back to Alt Moabit prison—my home for the rest of August.

Our court appearance was over, but our trial was just beginning. There we were—four young men, rejected by their country, condemned to the harshest punishment. Almost everyone agreed the sentence was needlessly cruel. In any free and open society, we would have been given opportunities for appeal of such a vindictive initial judgement. But where do you go when you start at the top? Helmuth apparently knew he would soon face the judgment of God, which is why he spoke with such confidence and self-assurance. In his heart he was convinced that the course he had chosen was right in God's eyes. Somehow, he managed to go beyond the structured thinking and indoctrination that he'd grown up with to see the broader vision of truth that existed beyond the borders of our native country. His insight and intellect enabled him to grasp the true depth of the Nazi evil. It may be easy with the retrospect of history to see how bad the Nazis were. But to grow up in the midst of that environment, being taught every day that Germany had the best and finest government on earth and still to have the insight and courage to break free of the propaganda, took a man of a high and special caliber.

The rest of us were brave in our own way, too, for we accepted the truth when it was given to us and had the courage to do something about our convictions. But, it took Helmuth's writing skill and leadership to provide direction for our activities. Perhaps our methods of resistance were clumsy, but the essential message he conveyed was masterful.

As the days passed, the realization came to me that Helmuth was gone forever. The hope of a reprieve or a reduced sentence was still there, but I couldn't forget the look on his face as he pointed to the death row graffiti in our holding cell. He knew his enemies too well to hope for an escape. Still, I prayed that something would happen to save him. It was hard to accept that the carefree days of the Lord Lister Detective Agency were over. I could never get his face out of my mind—the impish smile when he told a clever joke or the quiet reflection when we talked of serious subjects. I felt such a deep loss at the thought of never again sharing books or having his insight into the meaning of life and the world. With him I felt so strong, without him so alone. How I missed my dear friend.

CHAPTER EIGHT

SWAMP CAMP

After a few lonesome days the excitement of the trial wore off and suddenly I was confronted with an awful realization—Ten Years Imprisonment! I started thinking to myself that I was just sixteen years old, which meant that in ten years I'd be an old man of twenty-six, with all my "good years" behind me. By that time my mother might be gone. I'd have no future success in employment because of my prison record. My friends would deny me and I'd be despised for being a traitor! Gloom descended upon me like a dark, impenetrable mist. Things soon got even worse, for that day one of the guards, the most hateful one, took it upon himself to threaten me with death by hanging. With a few choice expletives he assured me I would soon be executed for the heinous crime of betraying my country.

I felt I'd been delivered into the clutches of the devil himself and this was merely a prelude to hell. I felt alone and forsaken. In this dark mood I sat down to write a letter to my mother. In the letter I asked her forgiveness for the shame and sorrow I'd brought upon her and assured her I would understand completely if she chose to denounce me and deny that I was her son. I let her know that as far as I was concerned life held nothing for me anymore, and I hoped to simply disappear.

The letter must have travelled with the speed of a telegraph, for just a few days later I received her sweet reply. She had sensed the depth of my despair and moved immediately to comfort me. She assured me of her love and promised that I would always remain her son, regardless of what other people thought. She counseled me to find comfort and peace from the Lord by seeking him in prayer. "Try to get a Bible," she wrote, "for within its pages you will find renewed faith and strength to face the trials that are now upon you." She concluded by telling me that it's always darkest just before the dawn of a new day, and that I must have courage and trust in the Lord.

This letter had the same impact on my spirit as a shot of adrenaline upon a dying man. It immediately dispelled the gloom and gave me new hope and faith. The words of my friend Hans came back into my mind, "You have to survive!" With an almost electric shock I felt his challenge lift my spirits even more, and I resolved deep in my soul to do just that.

I determined to follow my mother's advice to study the Bible, and asked the guard if I could talk with the local chaplain. This gave him another excuse to harass me.

"So now you want religion, eh? Well let me tell you, it won't do you any good. You'll still wind up in Ploetzensee to be hanged!" Surprisingly, he did pass on my request to the appropriate authorities. This was a real treat for the chaplain. Because of the Nazi campaign against religion, there were few calls for his assistance. Too many people believed the Nazis' cry to live as "enlightened citizens who consider religion old fashioned and superstitious."

The chaplain was overjoyed to find somebody who was interested in religion. After talking with me for a little while, he gladly obliged my request for a copy of the Bible. I started to study it seriously. One scripture in Isaiah brought me special comfort: "Let the wicked forsake his ways, and the unrighteous man his thoughts, and let him return unto the Lord. . . . For my thoughts are not your thoughts, neither are your ways my ways, saith the Lord. For as the heavens are higher than the earth, so are my ways higher than your ways, and my thoughts than your thoughts" (Isaiah 55: 7–9).

This scripture reached my inner soul and touched me profoundly. Even though I didn't feel my activities had been sinful, I still felt distanced from everyone, including God—for here I was in prison, condemned and despised by my country, while my best friend awaited execution. With this scripture I suddenly felt that even I, in my desperate circumstances, could reach out across the heavens to talk with God. I felt that somehow, in his eternal thinking, everything would be all right and would somehow work to my ultimate good. As I pondered this verse over and over in my heart, I didn't feel quite so alone. I had new courage to go on, to once again communicate with my Father in Heaven. As I started to pray more earnestly, and to ponder anew the doctrines I'd been taught since childhood, I began to gain courage. His Spirit had comforted me, just as my mother had promised.

The days passed slowly until one morning we were called out of our cells with the news that we were to return to Hamburg. We left Berlin just twenty days after arriving. How our lives had changed in those three weeks! Once again we were assigned a police escort and a special compartment on the train, along with the privilege of talking with each other. Just as we'd had trouble talking on our previous journey, this time the conversation was even more labored, for as there had been four of us, now there were only three. Though no one mentioned Helmuth's name, everyone was thinking of him with a heavy heart.

No one had bothered to tell us what had become of Helmuth. We knew he had been taken to the Berlin-Ploetzensee prison, but we didn't know how he was or what was happening about his sentence. Jail-house gossip had been so insistent that the court would set aside his death penalty, we actually hoped he would be on the train with us back to Hamburg. Instead, there was an empty seat.

Our first stop on the return trip was at the Huettenstrasse Prison, an old, decaying relic. From there, Gerhard Duever and I were transported to the A Section of the Investigative Prison in Hamburg (the section reserved for prisoners already sentenced). From 2 September until 9 September, we spent our time chasing and exterminating bedbugs. Poor Gerhard received many bites from these nocturnal creatures, which left welts the size of a half-dollar piece all over his body. I must not have been as tasty, because I had just a few bites.

On 9 September we were transported to Glasmoor prison (a youth camp), where we rejoined Karl-Heinz. Glasmoor was located in a high swamp area to the north of Hamburg. The main occupation of the prisoners was to dig peat, which was cut into squares and then stacked up to dry in the sun to be used as fuel in the large furnace of the prison. It was a dirty, hot job that left the prisoners exhausted.

The three of us were lucky and received an assignment to the camp tailor shop. We were trained to operate a professional sewing machine that could turn out the hundreds of pairs of pants needed for the prisoners. At night we quartered in a large area called the Craftsmen room, which housed twelve prisoners—six from the tailor shop, six from the shoemaker shop. We each were given a small cupboard in which to store our personal effects. These included a dish cloth, a tin cup, a tin bowl, a fork, a spoon, and a blunt piece of steel which masqueraded as a knife.

The room was divided into two parts, one for sleeping, one for eating. The sleeping area featured six bunk beds with mattresses so thin they did no good at all. The eating area had a huge old table with twelve four-legged stools surrounding it. After reveille at 6:00 A.M., we had to get up and wash ourselves and make the beds in tight military fashion. The camp assigned two ex-military officers as guards to make sure the beds were made right. For breakfast we received 200 grams of dark bread (Kommisbrot) and a tin cup full of malt (imitation) coffee. After this we were called out for roll call, lining up according to our room assignments. The guards reported "All Present" to Hauptwachtmeister Schulz (head guard reporting to the warden), who then gave the orders of the day. If the roll-call got fouled up for some reason such as a prisoner not falling in line or not standing at attention properly, the whole assembly received drill instructions.

"To the horizon, March, March, March," came the order, "In double time!" Sometimes, to put a sadistic twist to the punishment, we were told to do the duck-walk, which consists of squatting and then walking forward as fast as possible. This ruined many a man's knee joints, including mine.

After assembly, each of the crews was called out by its guards to start the day's labor. The peat crews would drag off into the distance to start their toil. The master tailor would summon us, and off we'd go to our little factory. After a long, intense morning of work, we'd be escorted to our room for a lunch of soup. This soup was a little bit thicker than the soup we'd had in Berlin. Occasionally we'd even find some potatoes in it, but they almost always had turned black from being frozen. They had a sickly, sweet taste, but we ate them anyway. After lunch the master tailor returned us to the shop. At night we received another piece of dark bread and our proverbial ersatz coffee. The only break we received in our monotonous routine came on Sunday when there was a pat of margarine to put on the bread and sometimes even a thin slice of sausage. The day ended at 8 P.M. That was a happy time, because in our sleep we could escape imprisonment for at least a few hours. But, no matter how pleasant the dreams of the night, the sun always rose again.

So it went for about a month. The days seemed to melt together until I wasn't really aware of the passage of time. On 28 October, just one day after my mother's birthday, we were all shocked back into an awful reality. On that day Master Tailor Franken called the three of us into his room where he showed us an article in a local newspaper. Printed in bold, black letters it read:

HELMUTH HUEBENER, Age 17
From Hamburg

Who was sentenced to death on 11 August 1942 by the People's Court for "Preparation To High Treason In Connection with Aiding and Abetting The Enemy," with the deprivation of Civil Rights and Honors for the rest of his life, WAS EXECUTED TODAY!

BERLIN, 27 October 1942
The Attorney General of the People's Court

We'd heard nothing of our friend until this awful moment. All our hopes and yearnings were smashed. Everyone started crying as Master Franken showed us the newspaper. He told us how sorry he was to be the bearer of sad news and gave us a little time to collect ourselves. I was numb the rest of the day, overwhelmed by shock and grief. That night I couldn't sleep but tossed and turned on my bed, thinking about Helmuth. Just what did they mean by "Deprivation of Civil Rights and Honors?" Did that mean they denied him even the basic comforts and necessities of human life before he died? Did they treat him even lower than an animal? I kept seeing his face as we departed, realizing the torture he must have faced as they walked him to his execution. It was early the next morning before I finally wept myself to sleep.

It would be many years before I received any answers to the tormented questions of that evening. Only after receiving a copy of the trial minutes and the official report of Helmuth's execution did I know the story of his final hours.

After the sentence Helmuth was transferred to the Ploetzensee prison, which was the political prison where executions took place. His mother immediately went to work writing appeals for clemency to the Volksgerichtshof (The People's Court) and the Department of Justice. Amazingly, the Hitler Youth also made an appeal for clemency, recognizing Helmuth's youth and mental prowess. Even the Gestapo suggested leniency for Helmuth, debating the point of his youth and of his brilliant mind, which should not be wasted. They also warned of uprisings among the working classes of Hamburg, especially in the districts of Hammerbrook and Rothenburgsort, where the leaflets had been distributed.

With all this in his favor, how could he fail to be granted mercy? Unfortunately, the Office of the Chancellery of the Fuhrer took the position that there should be no leniency in the sentence. The final blow came from the Minister General of Justice, Dr. Thierack, who demanded (with the Fuhrer's sanction) "To let justice run its course!" At that, the battle was lost, Helmuth had to die. As a further indignity, they suggested that Helmuth's remains should be made available to the Anatomical Institute of the University of Berlin for medical experiments.

When the day arrived, the Execution Committee made a final visit to Helmuth at 1:05 P.M. to inform him that all appeals had been denied. The first prosecutor of the Volksgerichtshof read the justification for the sentence with a concluding statement that the Fuhrer refused to make use of his right to pardon the perpetrator and to let justice run its course. Finally, they informed Helmuth the execution would take place that day at 8:00 P.M. and that he should prepare himself for his last hours on earth. They also told him if he had any last wishes, he should give them to the prison guards. During this proceeding, Helmuth was held firmly in place by two strong prison guards.

Helmuth's only wish was to write three letters: one to his

mother, one to his grandparents, the Sudrows, and one to a close friend, Marie Sommerfeld, who was more a second mother to him than a friend. Unfortunately, the first two letters were lost during the bombing raids on Hamburg in July of 1943. These raids took the life of his mother and grandparents. Marie Sommerfeld survived, but lost her letter while immigrating to the United States. Since she had read and reread the letter so many times, she was able to relate its contents from memory. It read:

Dear Sommerfeld Family,

When you read this letter I will be dead. Before my execution I have been granted a final wish to write three letters to my loved ones.

I want to thank you for the letter you sent to me, dear Sister Sommerfeld, which they withheld from me. I also want to thank you for the many happy hours I was able to spend in the circle of your family. Please remember me kindly. I am very thankful to my Heavenly Father that this agonizing life is coming to an end this evening. I could not stand it any longer, anyway! My Father in Heaven knows that I have done nothing wrong. I am only sorry that in my last hour I will have to break the Word of Wisdom.* I know that God lives and that He will be the proper judge of this matter.

Until our happy reunion in that better world, I remain,

Your Friend and brother in the gospel,
Helmuth.

After finishing his letters, Helmuth had to wait alone for the long hours to pass. While no one knows what thoughts occupied his time, I suspect he spent much of the time in prayer and meditation. Finally, the hour of eight o'clock approached and he was summoned to the execution chamber. I now turn to the official account of the Attorney General to describe the final moments before his execution:

---

* It is customary to give (by force if necessary) a condemned prisoner some wine to drink, mixed with a sedative to calm his nerves and prevent any violent outbursts.

27 October 1942

THE ATTORNEY GENERAL
OF THE PEOPLE'S COURT

8 J127 /42

Present: First Public Prosecutor RANKE, as director
              of execution. Clerk of the Justice Depart-
              ment, RENK.

The above noted officers of the People's Court today visited
the penal institution, Ploetzensee, in Berlin, for the purpose
of executing the condemned prisoner:

HELMUTH HUEBENER,

Who was rightfully sentenced to death on 11 August 1942.

The Executioner from Berlin, Roettger, reported to the officers that he and his assistants were ready to commence with
the execution.

In the foreground stood a table which was covered with a
black table cloth, upon which were placed a Crucifix and
two burning candles.

The back of the room was separated from the rest by a black
curtain, which hid the guillotine from view.

The above mentioned officers took their place behind the
table, and the executioner took his place with his three assistants in front of the closed curtain. Also present was First Inspector of Administration, ROHDE.

The Director of Executions then ordered the condemned
prisoner to be escorted into the room. At 8:13 P.M. the condemned man appeared with his hands shackled behind his
back. Two prison guards escorted him into the room, locking
the door behind them.

The Director of Executions then identified the condemned
man as the one sentenced to death by the Volksgerichtshof
on 11 August 1942 and told the executioner to proceed. Immediately, the curtain was withdrawn and the three execu-
tion-helpers took hold of the condemned man, who was
calm. The prisoner showed no resistance when he was
placed before the guillotine. With his shirt removed, he was
placed upon the apparatus and the executioner removed the
head from the body of the condemned man via guillotine.
He then reported the judgment fulfilled. Total time used for
the execution was fifteen seconds

Thus ended the report of the demise of Helmuth Huebener. It was written with typical German efficiency, right down to noting the number of seconds required for the execution. No one knows what became of Helmuth's body or personal effects. But we do know that he faced the end with a measure of serenity, born, perhaps, of a calm assurance of the reality of a life beyond this one, and supported by the conviction that his actions on earth would be acceptable to God. While the world lost a gifted son, I lost a true and courageous friend. Had he not purposely drawn the ire of the court upon himself, I too might have faced the executioner's blade. Who knows what contribution he might have made to the world, had Hitler shown compassion. With his keen insight into world events, I believe he would have matured into a strong and respected leader. Instead, he rests as a now honored victim among the millions who died at the hand of the Nazis in World War II.

In the movies the story always ends at a dramatic moment like this. But time goes on for the living. So it did for me. With news of Helmuth's execution, I was left with a deep sense of emptiness. Yet, somehow this news brought forward a new resolve to keep going. I knew now I would have to make my own way toward survival.

During this time my mother composed a letter to the government asking clemency for me. At the very least, she asked, could they not reduce my sentence to less than ten years? Of course this appeal took time to work its way through the bureaucracy and back to me. The immediate officer assigned to consider the request was my own Oberlehrer (Head Teacher) at our prison camp. He was to act as a counselor to give me guidance. In view of the harsh treatment I'd received while in the various prisons, I was surprised that this man, a member of the Gestapo, would treat me with a measure of kindness. When he pulled my file, which included the appeal from my mother, he looked at me a long time and said, "You might not think that I am doing you a favor by turning down this appeal for clemency from your mother, but in your file I read a notation that says, '*Release through protective custody only,*' which means at the end of your sentence you will not be set free, but will wind up in a concentration camp again. I think

you are much better off here, and so I will deny the request."
At the time I didn't think very highly of his action, but later
came to realize that he did indeed do me a favor by leaving
me at Glasmoor instead of having me released back to KO-
LAFU with the Lange Paul and other such adult prison
guards.

How can I compare a youth prison, like Glasmoor, with a
concentration camp? The regimentation is the same in both
places, including stern guards, physical torture of the military
type, such as drilling or softening up the "troops," and an occasional late night beating in darkened cells. But at Glasmoor
there were no gas chambers or crematoriums. We also had the
benefit of being under the supervision of our master craftsmen who were usually better to us than the hardened guards
of the adult prisons. There the guards were long-term profes-
sionals who had spent a lifetime dealing with hardened criminals. Their methods were brutal and unfeeling. Our guards
and supervisors were men who had made some kind of mistake while in the military, which landed them the assignment
of prison duty. Having been civilians before the war, they still
saw us as young people who would one day be set free. The
contrast was significant. Glasmoor was a better place to live.

In a sense our prison was a small community made up of
people who provided support to each other. Originally, we all
worked in the tailor shop. Later, Karl-Heinz was reassigned as
a painter, Gerhard Duever as an office worker.

While working in the tailor shop, Karl-Heinz had a stroke
of good luck when Master Franken chose him as his personal
orderly. This meant Karl-Heinz had to sweep out the master's
room, make his bed, *and* empty his wastebasket. This gave
him the chance to take a glance at the daily newspaper, which
Master Franken always left behind, thus keeping current on
the latest news of the war and local events. Karl-Heinz would
report this news to us, which brought a welcome insight into
the world around us. In addition, if there was a really important story, Master Franken would sometimes read to us directly while we worked in the tailor shop. He wasn't
supposed to do this, but because of his good nature and sense
of humanity, he treated us kindly.

At least here at Glasmoor, we had something to do with
our days to keep our minds occupied and our skills alive.

Even though the work was hard and the food inadequate, it was much better than spending our days in idle terror. For the next fourteen months, this would be home.

CHAPTER NINE

THE TEN YEAR CALENDAR

The rising of the sun each morning brought a day of hard work and hunger. It was the thought of Sunday that made the other days bearable. On Sunday there were no work assignments or duties, so it truly was a day of rest. We had the day pretty much to ourselves. Once a month we even had the chance to attend either a Catholic or Protestant church service.

One Sunday afternoon I saw a fellow prisoner make a daily calendar for his two-year sentence. After it was completed he'd mark off each day as it passed, counting down the days to his release. It looked like a great idea so I set out to make myself a ten-year calendar that would end 27 March 1952. It took several Sundays to draft that long a calendar, especially without a guide to follow (accounting for leap years, days of the week, dates in each month). When it was finally completed I was very proud of my accomplishment and showed it to my roommates. Soon my Sunday morning ritual included a ceremony of marking off another week of my life in prison. It felt so good to see those big X's through the days that had passed.

My ritual was short-lived, however. During an inspection one afternoon, a guard spotted my calendar in the cupboard. "What's this for?" he asked. "It is my ten year calendar," I replied. "With it I can keep track of how much time there is left of my sentence."

"Listen to me, boy," he said. "I have seen many prisoners in my time and some of them created a calendar just like yours to keep track of their sentence. Do you know what became of them?"

"No sir," I replied.

"One of them went crazy within the first two years," he said. "And the other one just shortly after five!" With that he picked up my masterpiece and tore it into little pieces, saying, "I am doing you a favor, boy, so you won't go insane yourself."

He then went on to say that a prisoner had to live from day to day. To focus on the long-range was to invite emotional disaster. A prisoner had to worry about that day only and how to survive in it, trusting that tomorrow will take care of itself. "That," he said, "was the only way to live and survive."

At first I did not like the guard for tearing up my calendar, but as I thought about it, I realized he made sense. After meeting some of the prisoners he talked about, I saw that he was right. It was better to concentrate on one day at a time.

My life in prison ranged from the routine to the bizarre. As one of the tailors, it was my job to produce or repair the clothing worn by those in camp. The largest amount of work was furnished by the peat crews, since they had to work out in the field. Needless to say, their work caused a lot of wear and tear on their clothing. We put patches on threadbare knees and sewed sleeves back on jackets after they had been torn loose by some strenuous exertion. Fortunately, we didn't have to work on the clothing until it had been to the camp laundry. In fact, our work in the tailor shop provided us an extra benefit—we had our clothes laundered weekly, instead of every other week like all the others.

We also had the responsibility of fabricating new uniforms. Every other month the master tailor would get a big roll of fabric down and cut out about twenty pairs of pants and jackets for prisoner uniforms. It was certainly more interesting to sew together new uniforms than to repair the old ones. Best of all, we could make our own uniforms. They were custom designed with oversize belt loops, creases, and extra pockets. Without question, we were the most stylishly dressed in camp—if prison garb can be stylish.

Outside the prison, everything was being rationed because of the war, including food, clothing, and shoes. It was understandable then, that the guards turned to Master Franken for help in looking the best they could. One of the services we provided was to press their civilian clothes each week for Sunday. Of course that also gave us the chance to press our own clothes.

As the war wore on, the material in the guards' personal clothing grew thinner. One day Master Franken suggested to the guards that they have us turn their clothes inside out so the material wouldn't show the wear as much. They happily agreed, and we had a new work assignment. The process was something like this: the material was very carefully separated with a razor blade, with special care to make certain we cut only the thread in the seams, not the surrounding cloth; next, we brushed out all lint and thread remnants; finally, the pieces were washed and pressed, with special attention to the seams. Once the material was prepared, we stitched the garment back together, but with the fresh side of the material facing out.

Once, I got mixed up and reversed two of the pieces, so that the left front leg piece turned up on the right side of a pair of pants. I sewed it together that way and presented it to the master tailor for inspection. He burst out laughing and told me, "Rudi, I want you to form a picture in your mind of this fellow running frantically to the rest room, trying to undo his fly—I'm afraid he'll have an accident before he can figure out the reverse sequence of his buttons!" I had to correct my mistake by weaving the button holes closed and setting the buttons on the proper side.

Occasionally, one of the guards was able to obtain new material in the black market. He'd bring it to our shop to have it sewn into a new suit. Only the master tailor was allowed to work on these projects. One day a guard, whose last name was Pape, showed up with an old top coat, asking that it be turned into a smoking jacket. Mr. Franken looked around the room and stopped at me, saying, "Wobbe, I think it is your turn to make this one. I'll help you with it."

What a challenge! I sat down, pulled out my reliable razor blade, and carefully started to separate the seams. After I had the pieces spread out on the cutting table, Master Franken cut the sides, back, and sleeves. He also reduced the size of the collar and lapels. I worked on this jacket for more than three weeks, turning to Master Franken frequently for advice and help. We had a couple of preliminary fittings before I finally had it tailored properly. On the final fitting, Pape declared that he was well pleased with his smoking jacket, and so was Master Franken. I was relieved and proud.

I wondered if Pape could ever have afforded to have such a project completed by a regular tailor, without the free services of a prisoner. He was very appreciative of my efforts, however, and promised that if I ever needed something I should come to him and he would do all in his power to get it for me. He also left a food packet for me with Mr. Franken which I was able to eat in secret, locked in Master Franken's room. This was the only time I was privileged to eat some decent food while in prison. What a feast! Food had never tasted so good.

The hunger we suffered in prison wasn't the result of a food shortage. Before being turned into a prison, the camp had been a farm estate. Because the prison was to be completely self-sustaining, it raised crops for vegetables, cows for milk, and pork for meat. The meat and choice vegetables always went to the guards, however, with the leftover remnants finding their way into our soup. It was real torture to pass by the kitchen when they were cooking a roast or steaks for the guards. The temptation was strong to linger. Unfortunately there was a kitchen guard, Oberwachtmeister Moehle, who was the king of all the food supplies. He had what we wanted most—food! He shared his treasure sparingly.

The prisoners who worked in the kitchen tried to help out by putting some still edible scraps of food into the waste drums where the rest of us could retrieve them. But when guard Moehle saw one of the prisoners lingering close to the door, he would grab a butcher knife and throw it at him. He never hit anybody but he certainly scared us away.

One might think that Christmas would bring a special treat of food or drink for dinner, but it wasn't so. Christmas dinner consisted of our standard fare: bread, cabbage soup, and a cup of malt coffee.

Because food was so scarce, it was the most sought after item on the camp underground market. The currency to barter for food was chewing tobacco. There were several reasons for its popularity. In addition to chewing it, one could cut it into extremely small slices, about $1/_{64}$ of an inch thick, and then fluff it up to use in a newspaper cigarette.

To make such a cigarette, the prisoner cut a piece of clean paper (a piece without newsprint) and rolled it into a six-inch tube that tapered from one end to the other. By crimping one end together, he had a makeshift cigarette. Once created, it was another challenge to find a way to light it. The best way was to find a small piece of cloth, preferably linen, which could be lit by striking a piece of metal against the cement floor. Once the material ignited, the cigarette could be lit. The smoldering material would be quickly snuffed out and stored so it could be used again later. Smoking was so popular because it could dull the ache of hunger that was our constant companion. I became hungry enough to use it also.

One centimeter of chewing tobacco would purchase 200 grams of bread (equal to a full morning ration). Because of its high value, my mother took the risk of bringing me several rolls of it on her monthly visits. Outside the prison, tobacco was sold in two-inch rolls that consisted of one-quarter inch strings, twenty-five inches long. Together they formed a roll about three-quarters of an inch thick. Mother would sneak such a roll into the prison visiting area, and then pass it to me under the table while we talked. Meanwhile, I'd be feeding it into the extra-wide belt loops I'd sewn into my pants. When the guards checked me later, they never noticed the roll underneath the belt loops. Each time I received one of these rolls, I felt like a wealthy man. I never got to keep it all for my own use, though. One of the first responsibilities of one who had acquired such treasure was to pay off the people in his own room. Otherwise, they'd report him.

One of the best ways to spend your tobacco was to trade it to the farm workers who had access to shredded sugar beets from the sugar factory. These shreds were sweet and tasty and provided a welcome change of pace for our diet.

One day I was so hungry I ate some food that had been prepared for the animals in the barn. I soon developed severe nausea, but was told I'd have to wait until the afternoon to see a medic. In the meantime, I was sent to my room to lie down. While I was on my bed another prisoner entered the room. He was a deaf-mute who worked in the shoemaker shop. He was known throughout camp for his fierce temper, which had brought him into the prison. (In a fit of uncontrollable anger he had killed his employer. For this crime he had received a seven year prison sentence.) He didn't notice me at first, and so went straight over to the prisoners' cupboards to find something to steal. When he got to my cupboard he found the piece of bread I had put there that morning because of my stomachache, but hoped to eat later in the day.

As he started to eat my bread I forgot about my stomach pains and jumped out of bed to confront him. I told him through sign language that he was stealing my bread and I wanted it back, but he just turned his back and ignored me. I grabbed him by the arm and turned him back around to face me, and told him again he should stop, because he was stealing my bread. (In prison, stealing from another prisoner was treated as a capital offense, punishable by ten to twelve belt lashes from each prisoner in the room.) This time he pushed me away. I became very angry and shoved him back. He attacked me with surprising ferocity. Fortunately, my boxing training came back to me and I started to defend myself properly. After I delivered a couple of good punches to his face he became violent and charged at me like a bull, but I used his momentum to run his head against an iron bed frame, which knocked him out. I breathed a sigh of relief and sat back down to catch my breath.

Suddenly, he came to and jumped to his feet. He ran to his cupboard, grabbed a long, pointed knife (an illegal weapon) and started running toward me. I sidestepped the attack and gave him a kick as he went by, which infuriated him even more. He changed the grip on his knife and came at me again, trying to run me through. I picked up one of the stools by the table and swung it around and hit him squarely on the head. This time he was knocked out cold. I stepped over him, twisted the knife from his hand, broke off the blade so he couldn't use it again, and threw it in the garbage can.

When I turned around I heard a voice from the window say, "Good fight, Wobbe. I didn't think you had it in you! Finally, someone got that no good troublemaker!" I was shocked to see the Master Shoemaker standing at the window and was frightened that he'd turn me into the warden for fighting. Instead, he came into the room and gave me a pat on the shoulder and said, "I saw the whole thing from beginning to end and know that you only defended yourself—and you did a darn good job of it at that!" Looking around the room he asked me for the knife. I fished through the garbage can and gave it to him. He then walked over to my antagonist, who was slowly coming around, and took him to the lockup cell. He was officially charged with possession of an illegal weapon and put in solitary confinement. Later, he was transferred to another prison. For my part in the fight, the guard never even put me on report.

Prison was full of interesting characters like the deaf–mute. The prisoners in my room came from many different backgrounds. Among them was a soldier of fortune, a confidence man, a burglar, and another murderer. Yet from the Nazis' point of view, those of us who were political prisoners were the worst of all.

Rudi Wulf, the soldier of fortune, was one of the most interesting to me. As a young man he entered the world of crime as a highwayman. His method was to cut down a tree so that it landed across a road. When a car came along, the driver stopped to see what had happened, only to be pounced upon by our roommate. His life of crime soon brought him in contact with the law. To avoid prosecution he joined the French Foreign Legion. After a series of adventures in that infamous corps, Wulf wound up in North Africa, where he was captured by the Nazis. During his stay at Glasmoor he made friends with another inmate called "The Mole." This fellow could crawl through anything. If he could get his head through a hole, he'd find a way for his body to follow. These two soon hatched a plan for an escape, which they successfully accomplished. As they were running through the field that surrounded the camp, the Legionnaire started to have trouble. As a heavy smoker who had been worn down by our prison food, he didn't have any stamina. About halfway through the field he started coughing up blood and had to slow down. The mole tried to help him, but Wulf told him to go on ahead. Soon Wulf was recaptured and returned to camp. They caught the mole a few days later. These two didn't give up, however, and tried yet another escape. Ultimately, Wulf was transferred to another camp, where he was executed.

Another one of our roommates was a fourteen-year-old boy who had killed his father with an axe. For that heinous crime, he received a ten-year prison sentence—the same I had received for passing out pamphlets.

One of the saddest stories of my prison term came from a young Norwegian boy named Sven. He was just fourteen when he was put in prison. He had a hard time communicating with us since he spoke very little German. Consequently, he was withdrawn and quiet. We often found him in a corner crying. No one knew how to console him because of the language barrier. I decided to try one day by using a combination of German, English, and my Low German dialect. In time I found out what was troubling him.

In addition to his parents, Sven had two older brothers and a sister. The family owned a boat and made their living by fishing the coastal waters of Norway. They would draw their nets into the ship full of a variety of fish, then sort them into different tanks in the hold. One day they pulled in a surprise—a downed fighter pilot from the British Royal Air Force (RAF). He was very weak from floating in the water for several hours before his rescue. It had taken all his strength to grab the net as it was being drawn on board with the catch. The family acted to save him, and soon had him wrapped in a blanket, drinking something hot to revive him from the cold. As soon as possible they moved him below deck to rest in a bunk.

The family spent the rest of the day fishing among the other boats, acting as if nothing had happened. When they returned to port at night, Sven's parents instructed him to hide on the boat so that they could take the British pilot off in his place. That way no one would suspect that they had picked up a passenger. All went according to plan, and later that evening Sven sneaked his way home through the dark.

Unfortunately, a Quisling Nazi (a German sympathizer) had watched their return to port and had spotted the British pilot in spite of the family's careful efforts at deception. The next morning they awoke to find the house surrounded by German soldiers. The soldiers ordered the family out of the house with the threat they would burn it down if they didn't respond immediately. All six family members came out with hands held high in the air, and stood anxiously while soldiers entered the house to search for the pilot. After an interval that felt like eternity, they emerged from the house with the British airman between them. The officer in charge immediately ordered a Summary Court of Justice (Standgericht) and sentenced Sven's father and his two older brothers to death for aiding and abetting the enemy. Sven was sentenced to ten years imprisonment. The soldiers immediately took the three condemned men and stood them against the wall of their own home, and shot them to death. One of the Germans then took a can of gasoline and doused the house with it. When ordered, he set a match to the house, and all assembled watched until it burned to the ground. The British pilot was taken away as a prisoner of war, having witnessed the execution of those who had saved his life.

It had been difficult for Sven to tell his story. It was interrupted frequently by tears, sobs, and a resulting struggle to regain his composure. I asked him what had become of his mother and sister and whether they had been shot as well. He said that they were alive, but had been sent to a concentration camp near Oslo. He hadn't seen them since.

I was curious about the German soldiers he had mentioned and asked him what kind of uniforms they were wearing. He told me that some were dressed in gray, but that the ones in charge wore black.

"Aha," I said, "then it must have been the SS who attacked your family!" I asked him if they wore the Death Head and SS signs on their uniform.

"Yes," he replied, "they did."

I then asked if they wore the eagle insignia on their left arm, instead of on the chest, and he replied, "Yes, yes, yes, it is as you have said; it must have been the SS!"

At last we understood why this poor young boy was so withdrawn from the rest of us, and why he cried so much. It was hard to imagine that for their act of kindness in saving a young British pilot from the freezing waters of the North Sea, his father and brothers had been murdered before his eyes by the ever efficient SS. Like so many Norwegians, he felt the sting of the Nazi viper as it occupied his homeland.

We inmates weren't the only ones with interesting backgrounds and personalties. The guards had their idiosyncracies as well. The first one that comes to mind was a huge, slow moving man called Wachtmeister Buhmann. Though slow of speech he was quick to anger. It didn't take long to figure out he was a cruel, sadistic man who relished his role as prison guard. His favorite saying was, "Ich heisse Buhmann und ich bin ein Buhmann," which means, "I am called Boogeyman and that is true, for I am a Boogeyman to you!" And he was. He acted like a monster sometimes, using his tremendous weight to terrify the prisoners. His favorite pastime was to chase prisoners around the court yard in double time.

Anyone who fell behind had to do extra drill exercises like, "Robben," where the prisoner was forced to lay on his stomach and then drag his body forward, using only his elbows and shoulders for propulsion. To sweeten this exercise, Buhmann would add his own enormous weight to the prisoner by standing on his back. He'd drive the prisoner on by pounding the butt of his rifle on the poor man's back while shouting, "My name is Buhmann and I am a Buhmann!" When so ordered we had to crawl in this tortuous fashion for the twenty or thirty yards it took for our tormentor to grow tired of his game. Of course Buhmann received great pleasure from this exercise, but the poor prisoner couldn't sleep that night because of aching muscles from the strain.

Another guard that everyone wanted to avoid was the Filzlaus (body louse). Nobody remembers his real name because everybody, including the other guards, called him by this nickname. He was the most hated guard in the camp, even though he never abused or beat a prisoner. He was a paranoid body searcher who constantly examined the prisoners for contraband. Every time Filzlaus came across a prisoner he would stop him for the purpose of searching every inch of his body. If he found something you were not supposed to have, he confiscated it and put you on report. He was especially notorious for this behavior after a prisoner returned from a visit with a loved one. After having your spirits lifted by a visit from someone you loved, it was particularly humiliating to have him order you to strip for a search in front of all the other inmates. Even the guards were irritated by his behavior, because he would sometimes stop prisoners assigned to their care to conduct a full body search.

Oberwachtmeister Paul Barth was a retired army captain who felt that the best discipline for prisoners was to drill them as though they were in the military. We knew we were in for a rough day whenever he was assigned to duty. He'd wake us up extra early in the morning and call us down to the court yard for exercises. He'd march us around with "Right turn," "left turn," and "halt" commands, then do it all again in double time. Then came the terrible duck-walk that was so hard on our knees, followed by push-ups and other muscle building exercises. An hour or so of this made us so tired we started stumbling over our own feet. Probably the most welcome word ever heard was "dismissed," as it was uttered by guard Barth.

After such a grueling morning, one would hope to regain lost strength by a hearty and filling lunch. But, alas, it was never to be. Cabbage soup was our only fare, and it was never adequate to the task of rebuilding our tired bodies.

So the days passed at Glasmoor. Outside the gates of our prison, the war was going poorly for the Germans. The early successes of the war, when Hitler could do no wrong, were now coming back to mock us as the Allied planes dropped thousands of tons of bombs on our towns and cities. In camp we complained about the food, but the truth is it wasn't much better on the outside.

CHAPTER TEN

TRANSFERRED TO POLAND

The bombing raids over Hamburg began to take their toll in the summer of 1943. Allied planes flew day and night. The Americans chose daylight missions in hopes of achieving precision strikes against the factories producing war materials, while the British flew at night on general bombing missions, using the cover of darkness to minimize their losses. For the residents of the city, the effect was uninterrupted terror twenty-four hours a day. As the weeks dragged on, the intensity of the bombings left so much of Hamburg burning that the heavy haze of smoke shut out the sun. The stench of burning flesh and homes even reached us in Glasmoor prison, some thirty kilometers from the center of Hamburg.

Everyone at the camp was worried about the safety of their loved ones. Some of the guards actually left their posts to travel into the city to find their families. On their return, they described what they had seen. Whole sections of the city had been destroyed, leaving the residents either dead or homeless. I was worried about my mother, but had to wait several months before finally receiving a letter telling me she was still alive.

Orders were issued in the last week of April 1944 to ship every prisoner in the camp to Poland. We were herded into a string of railroad cars that was to become our home for the next two days. The train's movements were painfully slow because of continuous strafing runs by low flying Allied planes or debris on the track. While waiting in one station, we could see boxcars filled with Jews on a track that ran parallel to ours.

Rumors were going wild throughout Germany about terrible things happening at places like the Treblinka, Bergen-Belsen, and Auschwitz Concentration Camps. In spite of the veil of secrecy surrounding these places, we still learned much through the camp grapevine. Yet, many of the German people turned their heads and pretended they never knew what was going on in these death camps. Others were afraid to say anything, for fear of their own lives being endangered.

Two days after departing Hamburg, we arrived in Graudenz, West Prussia (now Poland). We marched through the town toward the airport, where the camp was located. There were ten to fifteen barracks arranged in different patterns throughout the camp. I was placed in Barrack No. 3, right by the main gate. To my surprise, there were no SS guards, only Justice Department guards. Most of these were former professional soldiers who had at least twelve years of service. At first it seemed a relief not to be under the watch of the dreaded SS, but I later learned that some of these men were even worse. Fortunately, our Camp Commander, Oberregierungsrat Dr. Krueger (First Privy Counselor) turned out to be a decent man. My first assignment in the new camp was again that of tailor. As soon as I learned of the work going on in the airplane factory, I applied for a permit to work in their shops. This seemed like a chance to get back into my trade as a machinist. It was a great day when my application for transfer was approved, allowing me to become a member of the shop crew. Right from the start, I enjoyed my work there.

I was placed in a body-repair crew that was assigned to repair shot-up fuselages of the Messerschmitt 109 fighter plane. Among my workmates were civilians, Germans, and Poles. My job was to rivet patches over bullet holes that had been shot in the airplane body, replace shot-up gas tanks, and check the accelerator linkage and all the connections to the engine. It was quite a shock the first time I saw one of the gas tanks, which was shaped like a big easy-chair for the pilot to sit on. Imagine riding into battle atop 450 liters of high octane gasoline. I later learned that the tanks were lined with raw rubber that was supposed to absorb the bullets and close the holes so the tanks wouldn't leak. I was impressed by the 1400 pounds of the Jumo 211, 12 cylinder engine that powered the airplane. This was the same engine that powered the famous Stuka dive bomber. What a thrill to work on such a powerful, precision machine.

I enjoyed the work so much and worked so hard that in just six months I was promoted to the final inspection station, where I was able to work with the test pilots. I got so friendly with one of the pilots that he actually invited me to take a test flight with him in one of the training planes. I was more than willing to take him up on his offer, but one of the guards, a Nazi, learned of it and put a stop to my plans. He called me a communist and a traitor and accused me of trying to escape. I was promptly marched back to the Camp Commander. After Dr. Krueger learned what had really happened, he dismissed the charges, much to my relief. Angered by his commander's leniency, the guard accused Dr. Krueger of shielding me and called the Gestapo to investigate. Agents came to the camp and wanted to transport all of us in the Huebener group to one of the extermination camps like Treblinka or Auschwitz, but Dr. Krueger stood his ground and refused to turn us over to the Gestapo. I owe my life to his courageous refusal to cooperate.

It didn't take the Allied bombers long to find the airfield and factory in Graudenz. After a couple of bombing raids, the plant managers decided to move the rebuilding facilities of the airplane factory to safer quarters. Someone remembered the old fortress, Corbiere, on the outskirts of Graudenz, which had served as a bastion against Napoleon in the nineteenth century and suggested it might provide the needed shelter. In the casemates below the ground where the walls were six feet thick, they found a secure place for the repair facilities.

It was there I made friends with Thaddius Dombrowsky, who was a member of the Polish Underground. He had also been drafted to repair the planes. He tried to talk me into sabotaging the planes while we were working on them, but I just couldn't do it. As much as I hated the Nazi regime, I couldn't bring myself to willfully kill the airmen who flew the planes. Many of them, like some of my relatives and friends, were not Nazis, but had been drafted into wartime service.

My unwillingness to cooperate could have destroyed our relationship, but Thaddius said he respected my views and we remained friends. He was a good friend and a brave man. At one time he offered to send a letter to my mother over his address, which I did. In reply, I received a packet with some goodies from home. He smuggled it into the camp and I shared it with him. In doing this he was endangering his very life.

One day Thaddius took me aside and said he had contacted the Polish Underground to help me escape the camp and hide in Poland. After thinking about his offer for a couple of days, I turned him down. As much as I wanted out, I knew full well that my family would be arrested if I escaped. The Nazis believed that everyone in the family should bear the guilt of one family member. My conviction had already thwarted the career of one uncle. He was in the middle of Officers Training School when the commandant called him in and said, "Your nephew, Rudolf Wobbe, is in a concentration camp, charged with Preparation to High Treason, and herewith you are not worthy to be an officer in the German Army."

My sentence of ten years in prison wasn't enough for some people, and they tried to add to my troubles. One day one of my workmates asked me to do him a favor by taking his self-made cigarette lighter out of the factory for him. I hesitated because it was a serious crime to carry a concealed object that could be construed as a weapon, but still being a little gullible I agreed. I put the lighter in my pocket and walked into the yard in front of the factory. I knew I had been set up when the same guard who had reported Dr. Krueger walked directly up to me and told me to empty my pockets. I was given five days of bread and water in an isolation cell for my misconduct. The guard also ordered the barber to shave my head bald to further my humiliation. Much to the chagrin of the guard, however, I wore my new haircut with pride and enjoyment. It was my badge of courage. The other prisoners supported me by laughing and joking about my haircut, rather than acting like I'd done something wrong. Whenever this guard was present, they'd ask me to remove my cap so they could see my haircut, and then they'd break out clapping and cheering.

The prisoner who betrayed me received punishment for his actions too—but by his fellow prisoners, not the guards. One evening they waited until after the prisoners had been locked in for the night and the guards had left and gave him such a beating that he had to report to sick bay the following morning. The unwritten law of the camp was that no one was ever to be a stoolie and inform on or set up a fellow prisoner

During the time we spent in prison, my friend Karl-Heinz Schnibbe had been working as a painter in the paint booth of the factory. We did not see much of each other but tried to keep in touch whenever possible. He didn't have much trouble getting along because he was adaptable and had learned how to blend into the routine of prison life.

The food in Graudenz was passable, due to the fact that we were working in the airplane factory, which qualified us for better rations. All in all, this assignment wasn't bad, thanks to the camp commander, Dr. Krueger. While in this camp we learned that things were going even worse for the Germans. The Russian campaign had been disastrous and the troops were in retreat. After the spectacular gains the German Army had made in its initial thrust, Hitler had ordered it to continue their advance and take possession of the oil fields. To do this it had to conquer Stalingrad. This was one of the greatest mistakes of the war. By forcing the Sixth Army to march forward into this Russian stronghold, Hitler left their flank exposed. It was soon cut by the Russians. Nearly four hundred thousand Germans were surrounded in Stalingrad. When the field commander, General Paulus, asked for permission to surrender, Hitler demanded that they fight to the last man. After two hundred thousand Germans had been killed, Paulus surrendered. This he did in spite of the fact that Hitler had promoted him to Field Marshal (reminding Paulus that no Field Marshal in German history had ever surrendered). Fortunately, the general had the common sense to save at least part of his men. The Fuhrer would have destroyed the entire army. The last plane flew out of Stalingrad in January of 1944 with seven bags of soldiers' letters, but none were ever delivered. The mail was seized by the army and reviewed to determine troop morale. The high command hoped to find approval from the men doing the fighting so they could publicize it to the country. But well over half of the letters were critical of the leadership. A third were indifferent, and only two percent approved of the way the high command was conducting the campaign.

The report was canceled, and the letters, after the names of senders and the addresses had been removed, went into army archives. The letters were found in 1954 never having reached the loved ones for whom they were intended (Source, U.S. Document Center).

After nine months in Poland, another new year rolled around. It was January 1945; the war had dragged on for over five years. I celebrated the new year by going to sick bay for a week with a bad infection from a large carbuncle on my neck. I had a high fever and was assigned to stay in bed.

On the evening of the twenty-first, I awoke at four o'clock in the morning because of an unusual commotion in the camp. From my window I could see guards running about frantically, shouting orders at the prisoners. In the distance I could see Oberwachtmeister Jaeger shouting orders at the kitchen crew while they worked feverishly to make sandwiches for everyone. A little later in the morning the office crew marched by my sick bay window, with Gerhard Duever in the lead. I heard Oberwachtmeister Eggers telling them to complete the papers for the immediate release of one hundred prisoners and transfers for the rest of us back to Germany. The only thing this could mean was that the Russians had broken through, and we would have to evacuate the camp and leave our work at the old fortress.

At breakfast we tried to worm some information out of the kitchen workers, but they were only able to tell us we were moving out that very day. Meanwhile, the shop crews were frantically building sleds that the prisoners could pull behind them. Over in the barracks, columns of prisoners were lining up to receive their civilian clothes and belongings to load on the sleds.

All this worked to make those of us in the infirmary very nervous. We worried that we might be left behind. At 11:00 A.M. we were ordered to report to the clothing barracks to get our personal effects, and by 2:30 P.M. we were out on the road marching toward Graudenz, pulling our belongings on the sleds.

Talk about a ragtag group of prisoners. There were some thirty or forty demoralized guards to keep the column together. They didn't really need to worry about an escape, because no one wanted to wander out into the countryside to be captured by the Russians. Those of us from sick bay were placed at the rear of the column to do our best to keep up.

I was fortunate to have picked up a blanket from my bed, which now gave a little shelter from the freezing cold. I was still sick with a high fever. After a couple of tortuous hours of marching I had no more strength and started to fall behind. Without warning I felt a crushing blow on the back of my neck and fell to the ground. A guard had come up from behind and smashed the butt of his rifle into my neck, right on the infected carbuncle. The pain was so intense that I fainted. When I regained consciousness, I actually felt better. The blow to the carbuncle had caused it to rupture allowing some of the infection to drain.

With the help of other prisoners I was able to wipe the wound off with dirty rags and snow and then bandage it as best we could. I didn't have a lot of time to work on it, for the order came to march on. But the fever had broken and I was able to keep up once again.

The roads were badly congested with farmers and refugees trying to escape the Russian Army. It was a pitiful sight to see their faces as they abandoned home and country. Their old farm wagons were piled high with their most important personal possessions as they began the long trek westward. We were fellow travellers on a bitter, frantic journey.

The weather was our greatest enemy on the trip. We often had to detour around a stalled military vehicle that was also trying to make its way to the west. Other times we had to move out of the way so an army unit could pass us on its way to the eastern front. The military always had the right of way. When we reached the Weichsel River, our guards found the only bridge blocked by the military, so our group had to move upstream and cross the river on the ice. It was almost dark before we reached an old village where they told us we could rest for the night. We were escorted to an empty dance hall, where we slept on the floor. Some of the local people were kind enough to spread a few bales of straw around to provide us with a measure of comfort. I pulled straw up around myself and, totally exhausted, fell asleep.

The next morning broke clear and crisp with the sun shining brightly. However, it was still very cold. At roll call it was discovered that several of the prisoners from nearby West Prussia had escaped during the night to return home. The guards didn't seem too worried about the escapes because that lessened the amount of work to do. The going was a little easier that morning since the roads weren't quite as congested as the previous day. At late afternoon we reached the small town of Neuenburg, where we were quartered in the local county prison.

The guards let us sleep a little later the following morning, which was a real blessing for me. Then, much to our surprise, the guards told us to choose between our prison and civilian clothing. Most of us eagerly chose to wear our civilian garments. Our eagerness was soon squelched. As soon as we had made the change, the guards swarmed over the remaining clothes like vultures. They sorted out everything of value and bundled it up for their own use. They then told us several sleds had to be abandoned because of road damage. We would have to carry greater loads on the remaining sleds, including the extra bundles of our clothes that the guards had confiscated.

We were angry to think they had tricked us into giving away our possessions. In other parts of Germany people were being shot for plundering, but here our guards were able to plunder without adverse consequences.

With all the confusion of the exchange, it was almost eleven o'clock in the morning before we got on the road again. After a couple of wrong turns, we finally found the road heading for Preussisch, Stargard. On the previous two days we had been able to use side roads to avoid the large crowds. But since there was only one road out of Neunburg heading west, we soon joined the throng. Throughout the day we could hear the ominous thunder of artillery. It was getting close. Everybody was nervous and kept glancing toward the tree line of the forest expecting to see Russian tanks breaking through at any time.

On the third day of the escape we quartered in a large barn on an old agricultural estate. The many cracks and holes in the walls and roof allowed the biting wind to blow freely through. It was almost as cold as if we were sleeping under the stars. I was again able to find some straw in a corner of the barn. I dug in and before long was comfortable enough to fall into a deep sleep. I didn't even awake when they brought food later in the evening.

The next morning I was sickened to find several of my fellow prisoners had spent the night with their hands and feet tied with rope because they had been caught trying to escape. When I tried to arouse the fellow next to me to tell him about it, I found he had frozen to death in his sleep.

Actually, we were all in constant danger of freezing to death. On one occasion Karl-Heinz discovered that Gerhard Duever was missing, so he backtracked and found him in a snow bank trying to sleep. That would have been the end for Gerhard, so Karl-Heinz picked him up and brought him back to the group. We rubbed his feet with snow to get some life back into his badly frostbitten toes.

Whereas Karl-Heinz had a lot of stamina and determination, I was still suffering from the effects of my illness and had to drag myself every inch of the way. Even in the extremely cold temperatures my fever had come back and I was awfully weak. But remembering the words of Hans, "You have to survive!" I was determined to keep going.

Early the next morning we were awakened with the urgent command to start marching. The Russians had advanced far too close for comfort and we had to hurry in order to avoid being caught in the pincer attack about to take place. The guards forced the column to march in double time, a pace that I was unable to sustain for very long. The guards at last recognized I wasn't faking my weakness, and let me ride on one of the sleds occasionally, which helped a lot. In the late afternoon we were relieved to see the outline of the city, and everyone breathed a sigh of relief that we had made it. However, the wind came up and ice crystals started to blow in our faces—it was the beginning of a terrible blizzard. Even though we were within sight of shelter when the blizzard began, it took us almost six more hours to work our way around overturned wagons, dead horses, and the rubble of bombed out houses to the county prison where we spent the night.

The prison was severely overcrowded since prisoners from every camp in the eastern countries were being evacuated to the west. They put us down in the cellar and stuffed twelve in cells that were meant to hold only three. At least it was warm and dry and most of us managed to sleep even though we couldn't lie down. The next morning the guards found additional cells for some of the prisoners in our cell, which gave us a little more room. Because of the blizzard we stayed in Preussisch, Stargard all of the next day and were actually fed three good meals.

On the seventh morning of our homebound trek, we awakened to the disturbing news that the Russians had made another breakthrough and that we would have to evacuate the city immediately. Haste was the key word. Our group was able to make it out of the prison ahead of everyone else, in spite of all the turmoil in the prison yard. Once past the prison gates, we were engulfed in a frenzied crowd trying to escape the Russians. The citizens of the town had also received orders to evacuate and the confusion was unbelievable. To top it off, the city was attacked throughout the day by Russian planes, which shot into the columns of people while dropping their bombs. The winter weather didn't seem to trouble the Russian pilots as much as it did us. They flew no matter how badly the storm was raging. Surprisingly, none of us got hurt.

After we had cleared the outskirts of the city, the storm hit us with all its fury. We covered our faces and bodies, except for small slits across our eyes to see through. Armed with only a determination to survive, we pushed on but were simply too weak to make that day's goal. Late in the evening we found a barn that offered some shelter. I dug deep into the hay and spent a fairly comfortable night. In the morning, I found myself buried in a deep blanket of snow that had fallen through the gaping holes in the roof.

The kitchen crew, which consisted of Gerhard Duever, Karl-Heinz, and five others, did their best to obtain food for us during the trek. On one particular night they met with spectacular success by liberating a couple of pigs that a local butcher then converted into pork. We were able to carry the meat with us without fear of spoilage, since the winter took care of our refrigeration needs. I'll never forget how good our pork soup tasted that day. On this cold winter night our cooks were actually able to find some carrots and potatoes to cook with the pork, which produced one of the finest stews I've ever eaten. I finished off three large bowls of it. I was amazed at their ingenuity in finding the ingredients for such a feast. They were always on the look-out for something that would give us strength for the journey. We sometimes stumbled upon the carcass of a frozen animal from which the food detail would cut off a small chunk of meat to heat later over an open fire.

The next morning dawned cold, but beautiful. The sun was shining, the air was clear, and the snow had blown off the streets. It was wonderful to see the sun shining over head, and our attitudes brightened with it. The guards started the day by taking an inventory of our condition and determined those too sick to travel would have to be left behind in Neukrug. I was considered ambulatory and could remain with the column. Gerhard Duever was able to conceal his frostbitten toes and was also able to stay with us. Twenty-five prisoners were left behind to be captured by the advancing Russian Army. The rest of us, who now numbered less than one hundred, started to push on toward the west. Again, we found our effort halted by the mass of people and vehicles trying to escape.

The roads were clogged beyond belief, and we sometimes had to wait for hours at a dead standstill. After several of these delays a group of us who had very little baggage was allowed to move ahead by weaving in and out of the stalled columns of vehicles. We nicknamed ourselves the pedestrians. By nightfall we had made it to the next town where we found quarters in the local jail. It was late that night before the kitchen crew finally made it through. They had been forced to cut across the open fields and make their own trail, which took a lot more effort. Dinner was late that evening, but we were all glad just to see them.

The next day Oberregierungsrat Dr. Krueger told the clerks to draw up the papers to release twenty more prisoners. Only the worst offenders, like the Huebener group, remained under arrest. We still had to march to Buetow, Pomerania if we were to stand any chance of beating the Russian advance. Our chance of succeeding looked pretty dim just then, for as far as the eye could see, the roads were clogged with masses of people and vehicles. The citizenry was frantically trying to go west while the German Army was grudgingly moving reinforcements east.

On the eighth day out we'd about given up hope. After making a little headway, our group had been standing in the same spot for several hours waiting for the endless column to start moving again. Just when everyone had nearly given up in despair, the prisoners at the front of the column cleared off a snow-covered sign that said, "Buetow—17 km." Even though progress was slow, we again had hope that we might make it. It was so cold that if it hadn't been for the trees of the forest, the wind most likely would have thinned our numbers even more.

That night when the column finally got moving again, we found ourselves out in the open countryside with no protection at all. My group, the pedestrians, were told to keep on going, so we had to leave the wagon with our provisions behind, guarded by a few volunteers from the kitchen crew. We kept on moving and soon passed hundreds of wagons and trucks filled with refugees and their belongings. Once clear of the narrow passageway of the forest, we were able to make rapid progress. Although the wind was blowing, the snow had stopped and the seventeen kilometers melted away quickly.

Arriving in Buetow, we marched straight to the district court where we were greeted by Karl-Heinz and a couple of other fellows who had pushed ahead on their own. The thought of escaping didn't enter anyone's mind anymore. We all just wanted to make it back home to Hamburg. It was late afternoon the next day before the two wagons with our provisions made it through. They had been forced to slog across open fields and side roads to avoid the crowds on the main highway. They didn't have much time to rest once they made it to town, however, because we all were told to get ready to board a 7:00 P.M. train that was scheduled to leave Buetow in the direction of Hamburg.

The escape, or death march as we called it, was over. It took us eleven days to march from Graudenz, West Prussia, to Buetow, Pomerania. We started out with about two hundred and fifty men and arrived with less than one hundred. The penetrating cold stole our physical strength while the sight of mass human suffering wore on our emotions and spirit. It was only the inborn desire to survive, aided by the ingenuity of men like Karl-Heinz that made it possible.

Karl-Heinz had reserved a compartment on the train so we could all be together on the next leg of our journey. We settled into our seats with a collective sigh of relief and soon fell asleep, exhausted. When we awoke the next morning, we were stiff from sleeping on the bench seats but felt rested anyway. On that first night out of Buetow, the train only moved for a couple of hours before stopping, but we really didn't care. At least we didn't have to walk.

As the train moved west, we found that every little station along the way was organized by the Red Cross into a distribution point for food and drink for the escaping refugees. Whenever a stop came into view, we jumped off the train and got sandwiches, milk, cocoa, fruit, or whatever else they had to offer. Karl-Heinz always told the relief workers he was representing a group of refugees, so they loaded him up with everything we needed. They didn't ask many questions, just "How many?"

Our only fear was the field-gendarmes (Military Police) and the SS troopers. They asked too many questions and sometimes drafted men right back into the fighting forces. They were always looking for deserters and when they found one, they shot him on the spot. In our civilian clothes it would be easy for them to mistake us for deserters so we took a wide detour whenever the MPs and SS were around.

In spite of them we were usually able to get some food for our group of refugees. As the train stopped in one station, however, one of our guards, Hauptwachtmeister Eggers, ordered us to stay on the train and made certain that none of us got even close to the doors. He had discovered that the SS and Gestapo were on the platform searching for escaped Jews, and he didn't want us to tangle with them. His order meant that we would go hungry that day, but as he was looking out for our welfare we didn't resent him.

As it turned out, we didn't go hungry. Just as the train was about to pull out of the station, one of the prisoners noticed a Red Cross worker standing near the train. He opened the window and called out to her, "Hunger! hunger! We need something to eat because we are all starving here!" The poor lady was so shocked that she ran to the supply station and came back with a whole armful of sandwiches and drinks. After unloading them, she went right back and got some

more. We all snickered about our companion's chutzpa, but
he had gotten us food and that made everything all right.

At one station we thought we would have a long wait, so
we took Gerhard Duever out to stretch his legs. While we
were sitting comfortably at the snack bar, helping ourselves to
free sandwiches and drinks, the train suddenly started to
move. We jumped up and started chasing after it with all our
might. It would have been easy for Karl-Heinz and me to
catch the train, but with Gerhard's frostbitten toes he could
only hobble. Karl-Heintz and I each took one of Gerhard's
arms and ran as quickly as we could with him between us.
When we reached our car we lifted Gerhard up to the window and the men inside reached out to pull him in. We
grabbed the handrails and pulled ourselves on-board. That
was a narrow escape. If we had missed the train we'd un-
doubtedly have been shot as deserters, for we had no identification papers, or, for that matter, any money to buy a ticket on
another train. There was a deep sigh of relief as we settled
into the seats of our compartment.

For the first couple of days on the train, we were able to
get hot food whenever there was a field kitchen operating.
But that luxury didn't last long. As we proceeded west, our
train was stopped more frequently to wait for derailed trains
and troop specials. On several occasions we had to take a long
detour to avoid a bombed out section of track. It was hard to
find any food while stalled in the open countryside. Not only
that, but our train kept growing. At many of the stations we
found a small subtrain of refugees already loaded into their
cars. These were added to our train to help as many people as
possible escape the Russians.

When we arrived in Schlawe we received the news that the
Russian army had broken through and was moving deep into
Pomerania, which made the east-west rail lines impassable. The
only way open to us was up toward the coast of the Baltic Sea
via Koeslin, Kolberg, and then down to Stettin. This was defi-
nitely the long way around, but what other choice did we have?
We only hoped the Russians wouldn't beat us to our final desti-
nation and be waiting there as our reception committee.

We had been so happy to reach the train at the end of our
death march, I couldn't imagine becoming tired of it. As the

days passed with almost no movement though, we found ourselves getting frustrated. The delays were incredible. On one occasion we stood still in the middle of an open field for almost two days without any food or provisions. I shouldn't have worried, though, for Karl-Heinz just dug a little deeper into his bag and presented us with some sandwiches. They were a little stale, but provided needed nourishment. The man was amazing. He always seemed to obtain the things that were needed most at a particular moment. On the death march, for example, when we were all too tired to pull the sleds, he suddenly showed up with a horse that he called Belami. He found it at just the right moment.

The reason Karl-Heinz could find a horse and claim it for our use was because everything was in such turmoil that no one could keep track of anything for very long. We were in the middle of what has since been called a mass migration. Families were torn apart, mothers were looking for their children, children for their parents, and husbands and wives for each other. Everyone was caught in a giant crowd of people moving in one continuous mass down the highways. When a horse broke away in the crowd, it was impossible for its owner to chase after it. He was simply propelled forward by the crowd, locked into place by the people around him. His loss became another man's gain.

After what seemed an eternity, the train pulled into the City of Naugard, where a large prison camp was located. Orders were given that all sick and nonambulatory prisoners were to be left behind here, which would have applied to Gerhard Duever. Karl-Heinz hid him behind a lot of clothing and bundles in the baggage net so he wouldn't be discovered. Everybody knew about Gerhard, including our guards, but they all kept quiet so he could come with us to Hamburg.

When we finally saw Stettin coming into view, our morale went up one hundred percent. This was the place where we were supposed to transfer to another train that would take us directly to Hamburg. The orders were changed again at the last moment and we were rerouted via Berlin. Our train left the city just as the air-raid warnings sounded and American bombers began pounding the city. We would have made an easy target.

Our good fortune was short-lived, however. A couple of the bombers decided to find an alternate target and chose our train. Since a moving target is harder to hit than a stationary one, the engineer poured on the steam and tried to outrun the bullets. He pushed the old engine to its limit, gradually increasing speed to the maximum the tracks would allow. We didn't know if we were going to die from a bomb or a derailment. His maneuver worked, however, and the bombers broke off the attack and left us alone. The rest of the journey passed more serenely.

It was a depressing trip. Each time the train went by a large switching yard, I'd look out to see long refugee trains waiting on the sidings. I felt sorry for the people who had to sit out in the cold and rain on open flatcars that offered no shelter at all. When we passed through Berlin the following day I was shocked and appalled. The great city that had held such terror for me when I arrived for the trial had been reduced to a heap of smoking ruins and rubble. The occasional apartment house that had somehow been missed by the bombs stood out like a lonely ghost in the middle of the devastation. It was an awful sight. Everyone in the city looked dazed as they wandered through the streets. At last the train started to move again and we kept rolling until we came to Wittenberge, where our cars were switched and coupled to another train heading for Buetzow in Mecklenburg. Buetzow was the collection point for all eastern prisons, camps, and penitentiaries.

On 11 February, about the time we were thinking we would live on a train for the rest of our lives, we pulled into the Buetzow railroad station. It was my birthday. After a few minutes we were told to march toward the outskirts of the town where a large penitentiary, Drei Bergen (Three Hills), was located. Apparently this was to be home for awhile. At long last we were able to get out into the fresh air and stretch our legs. It felt great. As we helped Gerhard out of the baggage net, we could tell by the smell that his frostbitten feet were not doing very well. Karl-Heinz and I took him between us and half lifted and half dragged him up the hill toward the prison. As we assembled in the courtyard, the guards told us that the facilities were overcrowded and we'd have to spend the night on the floor of the chapel. Before we retired, they gave each of us new shirts and underwear. Not having taken a bath in several weeks, we were covered with body lice. In fact, we could truthfully say we did not have lice—the lice had us! The pile of used clothing we put down by the rostrum seemed to move on its own because of the livestock infestation. After we changed, the guards spread out some straw on the floor for us to sleep on. The minute we reached our assigned place we all fell into the deep, dreamless sleep of exhaustion.

Gerhard and I went to the infirmary the next morning to get help for our afflictions, but it turned out there were no doctors or interns on staff, just a medical orderly. I was in agony from the carbuncle on my neck and was desperate for help. When the orderly took a look at my neck, he said, "You belong in a hospital with that—I won't touch it." Luckily I found another inmate who had experience as a medic and was willing to help. By now the carbuncle had increased in size to where I looked like a hunchback, except that the growth was higher up on my neck. The pain from the pressure was excruciating. The medic said he needed a sharp scalpel to lance the sore, but none was available. A guard offered his sharp knife, which we sterilized over a gas flame and then doused in alcohol. I felt faint and was ready for whatever it took to get relief. The pressure was so intense that when the medic lanced it, puss shot out and splattered on the wall. I felt immediate relief and the pain, though still intense, was again bearable. After cleaning the wound, the orderly and the medic managed to find some foul-smelling, tar-based ointment to place on the open wound. It had some pulling power on the infection and started to draw it out. They changed the dressing three times a day after that, and I was surprised each time to see how much that awful black salve was pulling out. After a couple of days, I started to feel better as the fever came down. For the first time in weeks I started to feel like myself again. The cure was painful and left a permanent bump on my neck, but I don't mind; it reminds me of the medic who saved my life.

The food in this place was edible, but they didn't have salt, so it tasted bland. At least it was food, and we'd spent days without any. We were grateful to have nourishment to help build our strength.

Our group stayed at Drei Bergen in Buetzow for five days before boarding another train for Hamburg. I was grateful for the move because I had a feeling the war was coming to an end very quickly now, and I was anxious to get back home. Even though we had to get back on a prisoner train without really knowing what awaited us in the future, we felt a little lighter of heart, knowing that we were heading in the direction of dear old Hamburg, our native town.

As the scenery became more and more familiar, I experienced mixed emotions. I was grateful to be back in Germany, yet felt overwhelmed by the terrible destruction that engulfed the countryside. It was the middle of February when the train pulled into the main station at the center of Hamburg. Here, too, the war had left scars. After switching locomotives, we drove on toward Ohlsdorf.

Our train was shunted to a siding upon our arrival in Ohlsdorf. We had to wait there several hours before finding out which direction we would be going. This was important, for it would tell us which prison we were returning to, Fuhls-buettel or Glasmoor. I had no desire to return to Fuhlsbuettel, the home of my old enemy, Lange Paul. To my great relief Hauptwachtmeister Paul Barth gave us the good news, "return to Glasmoor." It was late in the afternoon when we arrived at our old prison. The odyssey that had begun nearly a year earlier had taken us to Poland and back, and was now ending right at the point of origin. It was 16 February 1945. For two weeks we stayed at Glasmoor with Gerhard in the infirmary and Karl-Heinz in the shops. My infection was clearing up nicely and had subsided to a large bump on the neck. I could live with that.

In the early days of March, several of us were transferred from Glasmoor to Hahnoefersand, an old youth prison located on an island in the middle of the Elbe River west of Hamburg. This time we were transported by truck through the countryside to the outskirts of Hamburg, where two motorboats ferried us across the river. Hahnoefersand featured one large prison house, two stories high, and several out stations for the work crews. I was stationed in the prison house since I still had over six years of my prison term left to serve.

What a change it was from the almost carefree and loose conditions we enjoyed during our escape from Graudenz and the Russians. We found ourselves again under rigid rules and harsh punishments. Even though it felt good to have been moved away from the chaos of the front lines, I felt uneasy and wondered, "What next?"

CHAPTER ELEVEN

THE ALLIES CLOSE IN

From the isolation of Hahnoefersand Island in the middle of the Elbe River we watched the war swirl about us. It was as if we were in the quiet, serene eye of a hurricane, while all around us the world was burning in chaos. The Allies flew endless bombing missions to destroy the harbor at Hamburg (and anything else taller than an automobile). In spite of fanatic attempts by Hitler's Waffen SS to fight Bolshevism to the last man, the eastern front continued to collapse. In the west, the last major German offensive at the Ardennes had failed to strike the desired blow against the Allied forces because the panzers (tanks) could not fully develop their fighting power. A traffic jam in the forest prevented them from reaching an open field where they could properly set up the attack.

Our world was filled with the constant drone of bombers overhead and roar of the antiaircraft guns on the ground. I had no idea what had become of my mother and stepfather. I had received no word from them since Christmas. Whenever I heard a new wave of bombers overhead, I said a prayer that they would be protected.

It took three days to get settled into our new prison and for the warden to work out a new schedule, but soon we were back into a routine. I was assigned to the farm, where I worked in the field spading up the soil and preparing the ground for spring planting.

The prison nursery still had some old seed potatoes and other vegetable seeds. Some of the guards brought their families to live on the island, and they established little garden plots to raise fresh vegetables. Some raised rabbits to supplement their meat supplies.

At the end of March, Oberwachtmeister Eggers asked if I knew anything about diesel engines. When I told him I did, he reassigned me to work as a backup mechanic in the pump station. My new supervisor was Mr. Hansen, a machinist by trade. As he showed me around the shop, which featured a small lathe and milling machine, he introduced me to the elaborate pumping system which consisted of a stationary four-cylinder diesel engine coupled to an electric generator which powered the electric pumps. The island had no fresh water and depended on subterranean wells. The pumping station would pump water out of the ground into a water tower.

In another room was a bank of storage batteries that could provide emergency power if the main system failed. As a young machinist I was duly impressed by this remarkable setup. On a hunch, I asked Mr. Hansen if he'd ever served on a submarine. He laughed and said he had indeed worked as a Machinist Mate 1st Class in a U-Boat in the first world war. It was obvious that our pumping station had been set up with the same care and caution as a submarine engine room. I knew immediately that I'd be happy working here and was grateful to be working closer to my chosen trade.

In my new assignment my first duty of the day was to go to the Beamtenhaus (guard living quarters) to clean out the furnace. I would remove the clinkers and ashes and refill the coal bin for the stoker. Next, I had to climb the tower to check on the water level. I enjoyed this assignment because it gave me a chance each morning to take a good look at the surrounding countryside. As I looked out past the fences of our prison yard, I felt a sense of freedom and exhilaration.

Once my routine tasks were completed, Mr. Hansen would schedule a work assignment for the rest of the day. Sometimes that meant repairing a piece of broken farm equipment or perhaps even a lock on one of the cell doors. Quite often I was asked to do repairs in the private living quarters of the guards, such as fixing leaky faucets, unclogging plugged toilets, or performing simple carpentry work. I really liked my new assignment and enjoyed the chance to get to know each of the guards and their families. Usually they had a special food treat for me after the job was done.

In April an army recruiter came into the prison yard to find more people to put in uniform to send to the front lines. At this point in the war they didn't care much whether a man had a criminal conviction or not. Karl-Heinz was close to the end of his term and so was a prime candidate. On this occasion they offered Karl-Heinz the chance to restore his honor by allowing him to join the army to fight for his country. Gerhard Duever, with his frostbitten feet, was excused from the draft and I was passed over because I still had six years left on my prison term. Karl-Heinz was released from prison and allowed to spend a couple of hours with his loved ones before heading to the front. Gerhard Duever was released a few days later, in part because of his crippled feet and also because his four-year sentence was nearly completed.

For the rest of us the daily grind continued. The only change was the increased tension in the air. Through various sources, we received reports that told of Germany's defeat on all fronts. Berlin was under siege by the Russians, the British Army was coming closer to Hamburg from the south, and the Americans were moving in from the west. One morning, while making my rounds, I looked out from the top of the water tower to see troops in the south moving in the direction of Buxtehude. I couldn't tell if they were German or British, or both, but I could hear the rumble of artillery every so often. Later, Mr. Hansen came in and told me the British were coming closer every hour and the front line was shifting almost daily.

The next morning the guards announced that twenty more prisoners who were nearing the end of their terms were being released that afternoon. As I watched them leave on the motorboats toward Hamburg, I had a feeling of deep apprehension, wondering what would happen to me. Would I be liberated by the British army or get shipped out at the last minute to another camp? I struggled in my sleep that night, fighting off terrifying nightmares depicting all kinds of terrible endings for me. When I awoke I found myself bathed in cold sweat and shaking like a leaf in the wind. That morning I knelt down and pleaded with my Heavenly Father to protect me from the awful scenes I had dreamed about and to one day let me return to my home.

On the way to the pumping station later in the morning, I heard a commotion on the shores of the Elbe River toward the south and hurried to get to the top of the water tower to see what was going on. When I reached the top, I was greeted by a round of artillery shells whistling through the air on their way to the other side of the river. The British were firing on a power plant that supplied electricity to the wealthy community of Blankenese, where businessmen and retired sea captains had their mansions. The shelling stopped after a couple of hours due to a counterattack by the SS. At least that was what one of our guards told us. He still believed in the end-victory for Germany.

That night at supper the guards announced that another recruiting drive was forthcoming the next morning. This time they did not let me stand back but put me in a line with foreigners and other long timers. After a patriotic speech by the recruiting officer we were told that a special battalion would be created for us and that we would have the honor of going to the hottest part of the front line where we could fight the enemy and contribute to the glorious end-victory for Germany. This noble action would restore to us all our rights and honors as citizens so we could start postwar life with a clean slate. It sounded grand and patriotic, but I wasn't impressed. I'd heard of these rehabilitation units before and knew they were nothing more than cannon fodder to be placed in front of the regular troops. Sometimes the men in these units were sent to the front without gun or knife. Their real purpose was to dig trenches for the soldiers that would follow.

I didn't want any part of this great opportunity, and decided to take a chance and refuse the offer.

"It's because of you that I have had to survive this ordeal for the past three years," I said. "I won't do you any favors now that the war is almost lost."

That was the wrong thing to say to an overzealous recruiting officer; he pulled out his pistol and started shouting like a stuck pig. In a shrill voice he screamed, "What do you mean the the war is almost lost? The victory is in sight and we haven't even shown them the Fuhrer's secret weapon yet—one so terrible that it will destroy the enemy forever. You are a defeatist and I should shoot you right now, you Schweinehund!" With that he pointed his pistol at my head. I thought this was the end.

Much to my relief Pape stepped in front of me and said to the infuriated officer, "Do not take him too seriously; he is sick in the head and does not know what he is saying." With that Mr. Pape dragged me outside to give me a tongue lashing of his own. "Are you crazy, man?" he asked. "Just what did you think you were doing in there? Are you tired of living?"

I was still in shock from the terror of looking into the barrel of a loaded gun held by a maniac. After I came back to my senses I thanked Pape for saving my life. It took great courage to step in front of that gun to protect me. He certainly paid me back for making the smoking jacket for him in the early days of Glasmoor.

The recruiting drive took another fifteen prisoners out of our group, depleting our numbers even more. I was greatly disappointed when the warden announced that all political and foreign prisoners would be transferred to yet another prison. I was the only political prisoner left and would be transferred with three Frenchmen, two Danes, and a Belgian.

I felt a deep foreboding about the move. In my mind I figured out that the only camp left in our area would be Neuengamme, the place where Heinrich Worbs was almost tortured to death. That afternoon I came across Pape and asked him if he knew anything about where we would be sent. I told him my fears of Neuengamme and that I'd rather try to escape than to wind up in that place. He told me to calm down and not to do anything foolish. The final marching orders had not yet been cut and there was still another option besides Neuengamme. He advised me to sit tight until he could tell me what was happening. Later that day he told me that the orders had been changed and we were all going back to Glasmoor in the morning since the British had just made another breakthrough.

In the morning we pulled out of the Hahnoefersand landing and after a day's travel found ourselves back in old Glasmoor. What a somber sight it was when we passed through the once beautiful city of Hamburg. Still, I thought, homes could be rebuilt and the city restored. We were still alive and the end of the war was forthcoming. A new life would begin and I could be a part of it. With that thought in my mind I reentered Glasmoor Youth Prison. Here, too, everything was in disarray. While everybody was acutely aware that the war was coming to an end and our liberation could only be a few days away, the guards still made us carry on our work and prison routine as though nothing had changed. On 5 May, the City of Hamburg capitulated to the British army. The grand war that had promised to elevate the German Reich to the forefront of world power and opinion had ended in a humiliating defeat at the hands of the Allies. The war was over for my city but not for me.

For some reason, the British didn't move on down the road to liberate Glasmoor. We expected freedom at any moment, and yet it didn't come. The days turned into weeks, yet nothing happened. Finally, one morning, some French prisoners decided they had waited long enough. As they left the camp with one of the peat crews, they broke free from the column and escaped north to the City of Luebeck, where they contacted the British army. As luck would have it, they found a detachment of the famous French Liberation Army that had joined the Allies after the liberation of France to "beat the Bosche."

As soon as the French heard of our predicament they immediately moved to aid their countrymen and assigned a small detachment of soldiers to liberate our camp. While driving down the road in their jeeps, they spotted the first peat crew, disarmed the guard, and ordered the group to follow them into camp. It was a funny picture to see the guard walking ahead of the column, at gunpoint, with a former prisoner holding the gun on him. When the soldiers arrived at the prison compound, they rounded up all the prison guards and put them into the cells, then gave me a gun to stand guard over them. I didn't like this at all and delegated my new found authority to someone else. The most important thought on everyone's mind was simply to find some food and get at the kitchen guard who had been so stingy with us over the past three years.

When a large group of the former prisoners arrived at the kitchen, we found that the German guard still thought he could intimidate us like he had done in the past. He flashed a large kitchen knife and ordered us out of his kitchen. This didn't impress a huge Danish prisoner, who picked up a three gallon bucket of split pea soup and dumped it over the guard's head.

By this time one of the French officers arrived at the kitchen and told us to disperse, with the promise we would soon eat to our heart's content. He then took the kitchen guard and locked him up with the other prison guards. He kept his word and that night we were all fed until we could eat no more. Talk about pure ecstasy. But for the next few days, we had to pay the price of our overindulgence as we suffered severe stomachaches. High quality food in large quantities was simply more than our digestive systems could take.

The French detachment that liberated us was soon joined by the regular British army. One of our fellow prisoners, Peter Montant, had been born and raised in Alsace, which is located between France and Germany. Earlier in the war he had used his education and fluent French to become a confidence man, which was the reason for his incarceration. He now saw the chance to play his old game again. Accordingly, he traded clothes with another prisoner who had belonged to the Organization Todd, a labor force that constructed roads and bridges under the direction of Albert Speer. This unit's uniform had the same color scheme as that of the French army. Montant used this uniform to masquerade as a former French soldier who was glad to be liberated by his fellow countrymen. Of course this brought him all kinds of special attention. His charade came to a quick end when the former warden passed on Montant's criminal file to the British officer in charge.

At the next assembly, the British colonel dragged Peter Montant by the ear to the front of our group where he said, "Here, is a first class liar who was trying to deceive the British army by pretending to be a French soldier imprisoned by the Germans." He went on, "While all of you will soon be going home, Mr. Montant will be locked up again to answer additional charges before a military court." With that he turned Montant over to one of the French soldiers, who kicked him in the behind, while the colonel called out, "Lock him up, and put a guard at his door."

At the end of May a commission of Allied jurists and officers arrived in Glasmoor to review each of the German prisoners before setting us free. We were asked to form a single line in the order in which our names were read.

At long last it was my turn to get a judicial review of the verdict given me by the People's Court, the Blood Tribunal. The officer in charge read from my file, "'Listening to BBC London and distributing handbills using the news thus obtained, convicted of Preparation to High Treason.' How very interesting" he said. "Why did you do that? What was your reasoning, son?"

"Well," I said. "I felt that the German people had the right to know the truth, the way BBC London was telling it to us."

He laughed and said, "Jolly good, boy. You can go home now, thank you." With that he waved to me to join a group of about twenty-five other former prisoners who were to be released. We were cleared to leave that afternoon but were told we'd have to spend one more night in prison before they could arrange transport back to Hamburg.

I don't have to tell you that we spent a restless, anxious night talking about going home, about how we would be received, about how bad Hamburg looked, and about whether or not we would be able to find our families. No one slept until the last hours of the morning. When morning finally came, we hurried to eat our breakfast, but still had to wait some time before we were invited to board a large truck that would take us to Hamburg. I had such an odd feeling as we drove out the prison gate at Glasmoor for the last time, free at last to follow our consciences.

It was 2 June 1945 when we departed. I had spent almost three and a half years in prison. When we arrived at the familiar landscape just outside of Hamburg, my heart leaped. I was free, and it felt good.

It was shortly after noon when we arrived at the Rathaus-Markt (formerly Adolf Hitler Plaza), at the center of Hamburg. The driver wished us all good luck, and with that we were left on our own. We each shook hands one final time and then went our separate ways. I started toward Rothenburgsort where, according to the address on the letter I had received four months ago, I would find my mother. But many things had happened during those months, so I didn't know what to expect.

As I made my way up the Moenkebergstrasse (street), I saw how the once beautiful street had been devastated by the tons of explosives dropped during the war. The once proud railway station now looked sad with its broken walls and windows. As I turned down the Messberg towards the Amsinkstrasse, all I could see was mountains of rubble and ruin where once tall storehouses and depots had been. My uneasiness increased as I came closer to Rothenburgsort, where the destruction was even greater. Here, an *unbroken* brick was the exception. As I worked my way through the ruins that had once been the Billhorner Roehrendamm, I almost choked up with fear at the thought of what would come next.

Yet, in spite of all that had happened to this poor city, the war couldn't stop the arrival of spring. My journey soon brought me into Trauns Park where I was able to walk between tall trees and green shrubs. As I heard the birds singing their cheerful songs, the fear left me. When I stepped out of the park into the open I looked across the soccer field to see someone standing in front of the Sporthaus, playing with a German shepherd dog. The dog broke loose and came running across the field, barking cheerfully as it jumped up to welcome me. I had never before seen that dog, Asta, but somehow she recognized me as family. By now my mother came running too, calling, "It is Rudi! It is Rudi! He has come home!"

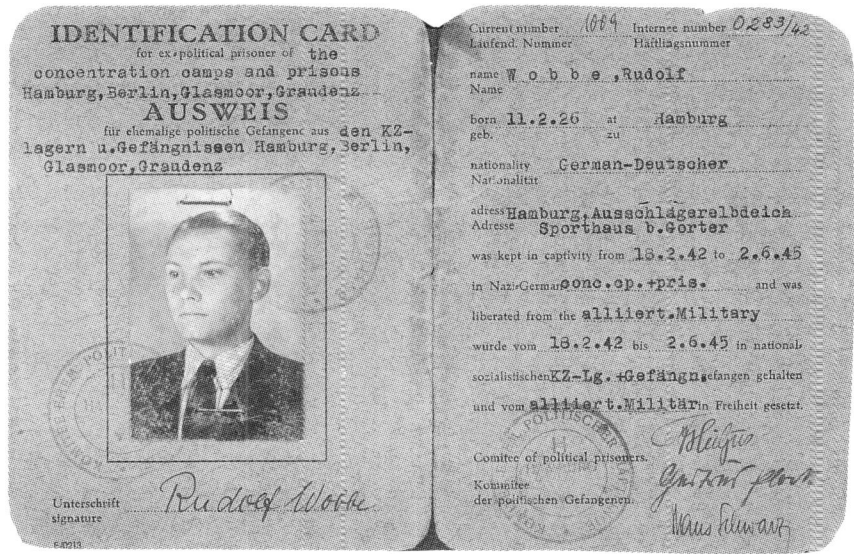

The identification card issued Rudi Wobbe after his release from the concentration camp where he was a political prisoner. He was held in captivity from 18 February 1942 to 2 June 1945.

The Three Musketeers, Rudi Wobbe, left, Helmuth Heubener, center, and Karl-Heinz Schnibbe all of whom fought against the Nazi tyranny.

Rudi Wobbe and his soon-to-be bride Herta Schmidt.

The Wobbe family emigrating to America aboard the
Italia. Wife Herta, Angelika (sitting), Evelyn, and Rudi.

CHAPTER TWELVE

PICKING UP THE PIECES

During my walk through the ruins of Hamburg, I had trouble shaking the feeling that I was really walking in my sleep and would wake up at any moment to find myself back in prison. I kept looking over my shoulder to make certain nobody was following to arrest me again. After all the years of hardship, freedom was just too much to comprehend. The anxiety melted in a moment, though, when I felt my mother's arms tight around me. We held each other and cried for a long time in a joyous reunion. My odyssey had finally come to an end.

I was surprised as my mother put her arm through mine and started walking toward the Sportshaus (Sports House). I remembered it as a gymnasium with large dressing rooms lined with lockers and shower stalls for the sportsmen to freshen up after an afternoon workout. Now I found it remodeled into four small apartments, one of which was my parents' new home. Since apartments were rare in the rubble of Hamburg, they were very fortunate to have such a place, even though it was small. The bombing raids left just twenty percent of the prewar apartment buildings standing in some sections of the city. The reason my family was able to have this apartment was that my stepfather, Jan Gorter, had gone to work for the Julius Luebeck coal supply company, which had received permission from the authorities to remodel the Sportshaus for their employees. This was a great fringe benefit.

Our apartment consisted of one small bedroom, a medium sized kitchen that angled into the hallway, and a small bathroom. It was large enough for two people, but a little crowded for the three of us. We were grateful for what we had, though, and made do as best we could. My parents had a couch in the kitchen, which doubled comfortably as my bed at night. It wouldn't have mattered if I had to sleep on the floor; all that was important was that I was home.

That first night together we talked until late in the night catching up on all that had happened during the years of separation. After my parents retired, I lay awake for a long time, much too excited to fall asleep. I'd pinch myself occasionally just to make certain it wasn't a dream. After a time of contemplation, I said a prayer of gratitude to my Heavenly Father for helping me come through the war alive and for helping me to remain true to our principles and beliefs. I fell asleep in the warm glow of a grateful heart that had at last found peace.

The next morning my mother couldn't wait to introduce me to all the neighbors so they could share in her happiness. I was apprehensive about how I'd be received, since I had been convicted of treason. To my relief, they all welcomed me with open arms and a hearty, "Welcome home, Rudi!" Almost no one talked about the events or party loyalties as they had before the war; the task now was simply to get on with living again. In spite of their poverty, all our friends offered whatever they could to help me get reestablished in civilian life. One might have supposed there would be great depression and hopelessness in this ravaged little corner of the world. Instead, I found encouragement and hope, and a determination to start anew in a world of freedom.

My other task that first day was to go to a government office and apply for ration stamps. Commodities were in such short supply that everything was still state controlled, making it essential for me to be added to the family's ration total.

Another problem was finding suitable clothes to wear. After all I'd been through, mine were worn and threadbare. But there was no money to buy clothes or any clothes to buy for that matter. My stepfather saw my dilemma and offered to let me share his wardrobe.

I was anxious to renew family ties and friendships, so we set out one morning to visit my grandmother, Alma Meyer, who was living with my aunt and uncle, Carl and Lisa Meyer. To get there, we had to wander through a wasteland of rubble and ruin that had once been the city of Borgfelde. My mother had to tell me when we turned on to Borgelder Street, because I couldn't tell where we were. Not a single apartment house was left standing in this once beautiful and modern section of the city. Yet I noticed people climbing over the ruins, only to disappear suddenly from the horizon. I couldn't figure out where they were going. My mother explained that they were living under the ruins, in the cellars and basements of former apartment houses. We soon came to a pile of rubble that had the name Meyer scratched into a piece of broken concrete. Mother led the way through a row of stacked bricks that outlined a small path through the rubble. Somehow, she found a flight of stairs leading to the basement room where my relatives had found shelter. What a wonderful reunion we had. I was thrilled to see my uncle and aunt and grandmother again. We had a wonderful round of hugging and kissing before settling down to do some talking.

My grandmother told me she had felt all along I would be coming back to them because of a strong impression she'd received while praying. She was a woman of great conviction and faith.

As we talked of the war, I asked how they managed to escape from the burning of Hamburg in June of 1943. Their answer was both terrifying and fascinating. During a bomb attack they usually went to a bunker right behind their apartment building. On the night of the most intense bombings, however, they felt a prompting not to go to their usual shelter, but to join my mother at hers. By acting on that feeling their lives were spared. Shortly after they left, a blockbuster bomb made a direct hit on their shelter, killing everyone inside. The bomb was so powerful it destroyed a whole block of houses and set adjoining homes on fire.

Meanwhile, they were having trouble enough in my mom's bunker because of an intense fire that was raging above it. The fire was robbing so much oxygen that people couldn't breathe. For awhile they were able to compensate by turning manual air pumps, but soon that wasn't enough. The bunker supervisors couldn't open the doors to let in air because the heat was too intense. Finally, in desperation they opened the doors to see if there was any chance they could get out. As good fortune would have it, the fire department saw them and laid down a curtain of water through which they were able to escape. Once outside, they started running through the burning streets toward the Elbe River. On the way they passed another bunker that had received a direct hit and saw bodies being carried out. After an incredible journey through the burning city, they finally made it to the banks of the river.

The noise and confusion and lack of oxygen made the trip a living nightmare. The sounds of a firestorm are almost impossible to describe. The wind turns into a howling fury as oxygen is sucked into the fire. The uncontrolled flames illuminate the night sky in a showering cascade of glowing heat and light that stings the eye and burns the throat. The fires burned so hot they reached 1800 degrees fahrenheit in some places, melting steel girders. And during all this the British Air Force was still dropping load after load of bombs. Truly Dante could not have created a more vivid image of the fires of hell than those experienced by the citizens of Hamburg on those awful nights in 1943.

Once at the river, my family joined a crowd of other terrified citizens who were also trying to find safety. After a short search, the group located several empty coal barges and hurriedly tied them together behind a tugboat. After everyone who could fit had rushed on board, the tugboat started pulling them upstream. Just as the tugboat reached the middle of the river a group of Allied bombers decided to make a run at them, firing machine guns and cannons. Several people were wounded or killed, but my family escaped unharmed. They wound up in a small town upstream from Hamburg, called Nitzow, where they were assigned to live with a farmer. Conditions forced them to stay there for almost a year before they could return to Hamburg where my Uncle Carl could continue his work for the railroad and my stepfather could go to work in the coal yard.

On my first Sunday home we went to the Menssen family garden house to hold a small Church service. Because living quarters were at such a premium, many families who had a small weekend cabin were now forced to use them as a main dwelling. So it was for the Menssens. We were all thrilled to have the chance to meet together and we were aware of how fortunate we were to be alive and participating in a church service once again. We were all grateful for the chance to partake of the sacrament, to renew old friendships, to be survivors. The joy was mingled with sadness, for it was here that we talked about all those in our congregation who had not survived the war or who were still missing.

Food shortages soon became acute throughout Europe. Even though I received a few extra ration stamps for having been a victim of Nazi injustice, there was never enough food to fill our stomachs. The only way for most people to cope was to trade directly with the farmers. Daily train journeys to the countryside became routine. So scarce was food that people would trade anything of value to a willing farmer. You could enter a humble farmer's home to find an expensive Persian rug hanging from his wall while his wife wore brilliant diamond rings on her fingers. Since my stepfather worked for a coal company, our trading currency was coal. On my first trip into the countryside we boarded the train with fifty pounds of coal on our backs. That night we returned with a hundred pounds of potatoes and a strip of bacon, a real luxury.

My mother used this extra food carefully, but we still had to travel out to the country more often than we would like. The reason for our caution was that the police declared it illegal for citizens to trade directly with the farmers. To enforce the law they set up inspection stations in the railroad terminals and confiscated potatoes, meat, and other foodstuffs they found on the smugglers, as they called us. I remember coming into the station with my uncle one day carrying a couple of bags of potatoes when a commotion started in front of us. A number of people were stopped by a particularly mean police officer who insisted he was going to confiscate everything they brought home with them. This threat started a small riot. People who are desperately hungry will resort to violence, particularly when they have traded away some prized possession to get the food in the first place. At first there were two police officers, one of whom was telling the other to let them go. But the first officer insisted he had to enforce the law, so his partner left him on his own. This was the opportunity the crowd had waited for. They picked potatoes from their sacks and started throwing them at the police officer. He finally got the message and made a hasty retreat. After this experience we always jumped off the train before it reached the station.

Later my stepfather was able to buy a used bicycle, a real antique with wooden wheels, for 1,000 marks. Now there were bicycles for both of us. The bicycle that my parents already owned had never been available for my use before, but now I was free to use it whenever I wanted. It's amazing how much brighter the world looks when you have the freedom to move around independently. I no longer had to walk or use streetcars.

One day a friend suggested I contact a new organization recently formed by survivors of the concentration camps called the Union of the Victims of the Nazi Regime (VNN). I did and soon learned that their goal was to help each other adjust to postwar life and to get recognition and support from the military government. As soon as I signed up I received 200 marks to tide me over. They also gave me some coupons to buy new clothing. What a great bunch of people they were, volunteering to help their fellow inmates. They also started an informative program for the general populous to tell them of the Resistance Movement that had existed through all the years of the Nazi regime and of its members who had been tortured, imprisoned, and executed for their efforts. Our goal was to constantly remind the world that these atrocities should never happen again. I was honored to join with them and made the effort to participate in many of their activities.

My ability to participate in anything too strenuous was still pretty limited, however, because of the devastating effects of prison life on my health. Not only had I lost a great amount of weight, but I also suffered from the effects of the infection and illness I had contracted in Poland. Still, I joined with my neighbors in cleaning up and searching for food.

We ran on to some good luck one day. As the city of Hamburg was cleaning up the demolished or burned-out warehouses, they discovered a silo full of rye grain. The inspectors declared it unfit for human consumption because of smoke damage, and ordered it shipped in barges upstream to be used as animal feed. Some of the rye found its way to my stepfather's coal yard for temporary storage. When he came home and told us about it, we decided to try an experiment. We obtained a sample, washed it and ground it up into a coarse flour which my mother baked into a dark, heavy bread. It had a smoky flavor, but tasted all right otherwise. With careful preparation it was safe for human consumption after all. My stepfather was granted permission to take a couple hundred pounds of the rye and we began processing it immediately.

My job was to grind the grain into flour. I shopped around to find someone who had a grinder. My uncle Carl offered an old coffee grinder, which worked well enough for small quantities, but would have taken forever on hundreds of pounds of rye. After a thorough search, worthy in every respect of the Lord Lister Detective Agency, I found my way to Brother Richard Pruess, a member of our old St. Georg Branch who lived in Rahlstedt. He had a large wheat grinder which he was pleased to let us use. I loaded up a couple of bags of grain and rode my bicycle out to his home to convert the grain into flour. Of course his generosity was rewarded with an ample supply of finished flour to feed his family. Once it was all ground, we distributed the flour to many needy families in our congregation. Although the bread made from the flour was coarse and dark, it stifled the ache of our hungry stomachs.

As more members returned to Hamburg, our little branch of the Church was growing stronger and bigger. We soon outgrew our cottage home and obtained permission from the Free Masons to use their old assembly hall. It had suffered war damage, but was fixed in a hurry—except for the open skylight. There it was, a great gaping hole in the middle of the roof which allowed all the heat to escape and all the rain and snow to come in. As winter approached we had to find a way to repair it. All attempts to find glass proved useless, so we decided to close it up. All building materials were under the control of the military government, which in our area was the British Army. While discussing what to do, one of our members spoke up and told us he was working for the British Army unit that controlled the roofing tar paper we needed so badly. Officially we didn't qualify for any, but our friend found an army guard who was willing, unofficially, to let us have three rolls. So, early one morning three of us waited quietly outside the walls of the army depot. All of a sudden three rolls of tar paper came flying over the wall and dropped at our feet, due, I suppose, to a specialized form of G.I. requisitioning. We grabbed our prize and raced to the subway station to catch a train for Altona where we would meet our branch president, Brother Herbert Baarz. Once there, he joined me and my companions, Walter Kindt and Heinz Bonitz, in making short work of closing up the skylight and securing the building from the weather.

The next Sunday everyone was a lot warmer during the meetings, particularly with the help of fifty pounds of coal that fed a large potbellied stove in the middle of the room. The water in the sacrament cups didn't freeze any more. Jan and I made quite a sight as we went to church in those days, dressed in suits, lugging fifty pounds of coal on our backs.

We had to do a lot of unconventional things, but I found early in life that the Lord really does help those who try to help themselves. It's only when one is at the end of his rope that the Lord steps in to help. It was certainly important in my life that at last we could meet again in Church on Sunday to receive spiritual strength. Our whole congregation and all religious people in Germany were hungry for the nourishment that comes from hearing the word of God.

Something of an amusing, yet pathetic, incident happened to me one day while I was riding a streetcar into town. I was standing on the back platform of the car when I noticed a familiar face in the crowd. I studied the man for awhile before realizing it was my old guard Filzlaus. In civilian clothes he looked quite different, but I knew it was the same man. He must have felt me looking at him, for he turned and looked straight at me. At first he didn't recognize me, but I kept staring at him. Then I smiled. As he started to smile back, I saw his expression change suddenly into a grimace of terror. The moment he recognized me, he whirled around and pushed his way to the front of the streetcar, which was moving quite rapidly. In spite of the speed of the streetcar, he jumped off and onto the street, falling down and rolling head over heels until he came to a stop in front of an oncoming automobile, which barely avoided hitting him. I watched him get up and limp away, still looking over his shoulder as if expecting me to chase him. I felt sorry for him, in spite of the fact that he was one of the obnoxious guards who had given us so much grief and humiliation. Still, I held no feelings of malice toward him and didn't really understand his fear of me.

I later found out that many former guards had cause to fear. I heard one day that my former enemy, the SS Guard der Lange Paul had been identified by some of the former inmates of KOLAFU. They beat him to death in broad daylight on a main street in Hamburg before the police could stop them. Perhaps that was the reason Filzlaus was so afraid of me. Unfortunately, there was a spirit of revenge among some of the former inmates of the camps who would not wait for justice to take its course. Not that justice was always satisfied. Sometimes the sentences passed out to the murderers and henchmen of the Nazi regime were far too lenient to redress the suffering they had caused.

With the memory of the Nazi atrocities and its high-handed and arbitrary justice system still fresh on everyone's mind, many in the legal system went overboard in the other direction so they would not be compared to the Nazis. Some time ago I learned of a terrible incident that took place in the last days of the war in a school in Rothenburgsort, located just across the railroad bridge from our home in an area called the Billhorner Deich. There, in an old school that had been converted into an auxiliary building of the dreaded Neuengamme Concentration Camp, the Nazis hanged twenty Jewish children on the nights of 20–21 April 1945—just days before the war ended. The children had been the victims of medical experiments at Auschwitz, and their murder was intended to wipe out all traces of those infamous deeds. Along with the children, twenty Russian and eleven French and Dutch prisoners of war were hanged also.

As terrible as this incident was, the War Crimes Tribunal that tried Arnold Strippel, the SS First Lieutenant who ordered the murder, pronounced a sentence of just three and half years in prison. In addition to such a light sentence for such a heinous crime, they declared that since he had already been imprisoned for more than that time, he was to be set free. No wonder the victims of the Nazi regime were sometimes driven to take justice into their own hands. As an appendix to this chapter I've included a translation of testimony given by a relative of one of the murdered children to the court. His agonized plea for justice went unheeded, but still stands as a witness against those who committed that terrible crime.

But not all our guards had been terrible. One day I was pleased to meet Hauptwachtmeister Eggers on the street while out window shopping. He was glad to see me and inquired about how things were going in my life. Since he seemed to be genuinely interested, I was more than willing to talk with him, remembering that he had been one of the good guards who treated us fairly. As we talked he told me about the ordeal being suffered by our former warden, Ober-regierungsrat Dr. Krueger, who had been suspended from his position while awaiting the results of an investigation about his activities as camp commander in Graudenz. He had been accused of crimes against humanity. When I asked Eggers about Dr. Krueger's trial date he said it was still pending, then asked if I would be willing to testify in his behalf. When I told him that I would, he asked for my address and said he'd stay in touch.

In two weeks I received a summons to appear before a judge to testify at the de-Nazification hearings of Dr. Krueger. I entered the court room with apprehension, remembering back to my own trial. I got up my courage and stood before the judge when ordered. After a few of the customary questions about my background, he asked how I came to know Dr. Krueger. I replied I had been an inmate in his camp from April, 1944 until January of 1945. He asked if I knew of any infractions of human rights committed by Dr. Krueger during his assignment at Graudenz, or of any pro-Nazi behavior.

"Absolutely not, your honor," I replied. "If anything, the opposite is true!"

"If this is the case would you please elaborate," the judge asked.

I responded, "As a matter of fact, your honor, Dr. Krueger went out of his way to help those of us who were political prisoners, sometimes to the point of jeopardizing his own position by favoring us over and above the other prisoners." I went on to explain that we were often given positions of trust and responsibility. For example, Gerhard Duever was assigned as a clerk in the commander's office, Karl-Heinz Schnibbe was made a painter in the airplane factory, and I was made a trustee (inspector) in the final assembly area of the airplane factory—and all this over the protests of the pro-Nazi guards.

The judge asked what I meant when I said that Dr. Krueger had jeopardized his own position by favoring us.

"Just this, your honor," I replied. "While still in Poland, Dr. Krueger told me that he had received an inquiry from the Gestapo requesting we be transferred to a local concentration camp. In spite of Gestapo pressure, he denied the request. I would say that's sticking his neck out for us," I concluded.

The judge smiled and said, "Yes, I would say he 'stuck his neck out for you,' and I think we have heard enough." He called Dr. Krueger to the bench and said, "I think there is no reason to continue this hearing any longer. With this last statement especially, along with the others that have preceded it, you have been fully exonerated and this court recommends your reinstatement to your former position in the Justice Department."

Dr. Krueger came toward me in long strides, grabbed my hand and shook it vigorously while saying, "Thank you very much, Herr Wobbe. I shall never forget this." We talked for a moment, then he told me something that made my blood run chill. "I want to tell you now that there were three times, not one, when the Gestapo wanted you transferred to one of the local concentration camps, especially after the incident with the pilot who wanted to take you flying. The Nazi guard who intervened at the time went right over my head and reported the incident directly to the Gestapo, who wasted no time asking for an immediate transfer. If it wasn't for your performance record at the airplane factory and the additional testimony of the director of the plant, I'm afraid my statement wouldn't have been enough to save you. To be honest, I still don't know how you escaped their grasp. Perhaps it was the God you told me you believed in during our interview. You said that he would protect you and it looks like he did."

What a great moment that was for me, standing by the man who had three times saved my life. I was grateful I had been given the opportunity to help him in return.

Next to shake my hand was Hauptwachtmeister Eggers who said, "That was very decent of you, Wobbe. Thank you for coming!" I replied that it was the truth and that Dr. Krueger was a very good man. I believe it's important to support good men and women and to oppose evil. That's why I joined with Helmuth and the others in the first place.

Following the war Gerhard Duever had a rough time getting his feet healed up enough to go ahead with his life. After a long recuperation period he applied to get his old job back at the Hamburg Office of the Department of Social Services. In view of all he'd been through, they accepted him back and reinstated him to his former position. Things were worse for Karl-Heinz. After being drafted into the army toward the close of the war, he had been shipped to Czechoslovakia. Before he even had a chance to do any real fighting, the war ended. His unit was in a Russian occupied sector and was arrested by the Red Army and shipped off to a Russian prison camp in the frozen regions of Siberia. There he lived under terrible conditions that almost cost him his life. He was finally released in 1949. Had he been allowed to stay with us for just three more weeks, he could have avoided the awful ordeal in Russia. Instead, because of the Nazis, he had to suffer two imprisonments instead of one.

The days and weeks passed quickly. There was so much work to be done in rebuilding our city that there was little time to fret or brood about what had gone on before. While there was much suffering and hardship, there was also a sense of hope and optimism. Having spent my whole life under the almost suffocating pall of Nazism, a government which gained its power and strength from repression, violence, and unbelievable cruelty, it now seemed the sun was finally shining. It was like walking out of a dirty, smoke-filled room into the crisp, clean air of a brilliant morning. We all felt liberated. In the fresh spring breezes of freedom, everyone thrived. After all the hardships, I was glad to be alive.

APPENDIX TO CHAPTER TWELVE

Testimony Given by Henri Morgenstern to the War Crimes Trial of Arnold Strippel:

We are here because we are the relatives of the victims you have executed. It is a miracle that we are alive today to testify to this court. It is almost unbelievable that there are even some of us left to raise this protest, because almost all the Jews in this country were executed.

I see there is a cross on the wall. Is not Germany a democratic country in which all religions are permitted? Why, then, is there no Star of David next to this cross? If I were to be arraigned before this court one day, would I have to swear an oath before this cross? There is a truth, a truth you know very well, that Germany today is Judenrein, [free of Jews] or nearly so. This immaculate country, with its wonderful meadows, fields, and forests, has looked upon the murder of Jews as simply a matter of keeping itself clean. Before they brought we Jews into the gas chambers, they told us with a smile, "You have to be clean, so take a good shower!"

Today you would like us to be silent so you can continue your kind of justice. But, what kind of justice did you show the world when, in this very room, you acquitted four murderers of Majdanek—murderers whose hands were red from the blood of our brothers and sisters and parents!

What a disgrace for your system of justice, and what shame the whole world feels for you who dispense justice in such a way. Who are the real victims? These murderers here, or the unfortunate ones they destroyed? We feel shame and so should you!

Then there is that man over there! Look at Strippel, this murderer who doesn't even dare to look me in the face, this coward, this murderer of children! My name is Henri Morgenstern. He hanged my little twelve-year-old cousin Jacqueline Morgenstern, together with nineteen other children in the cellar of the school at Bullenhuser Damm in Hamburg, in 1945.

Look at this murderer and how he hangs his head! What can we learn from him? Has the son learned anything from the father? Yes! he has become a member of the neo-Nazi movement. These people are dangerous, terribly dangerous. I am not speaking here to remind you of a painful past that continues to hurt us. I am speaking here in order to protect my children from the dangers that we have experienced.

Convict these murderers! Do it in such a way that atrocities like these will never again be repeated! If this court defends this murderer, or excuses his actions, it makes itself an accomplice to his crimes. For us, that would be scandalous. That's why we cry out here, and we will keep on crying out as long as we live, "Condemn the Nazi murderers!" We will cry out our demands as long as German justice does nothing to win our trust. We don't want revenge, we just want justice.

The former inmates of Neuengamme left a wreath at the school of Bullenhuser Damm which read, "Dear Children, we have not forgotten you!"

CHAPTER THIRTEEN

LEAVING THE PAST BEHIND

The performing arts were making a comeback in the city. School auditoriums were used at first, but in time the city rebuilt some of the theatres and stages. I was thrilled to attend performances of Pygmalion, Hamlet, and other plays along with recitals and concerts. One day an event took place that lifted the spirits of the whole city—the opera house reopened after major reconstruction (nearly two-thirds of the building had been destroyed by a bomb blast). The opera company started the new season with a performance of *Carmen* followed by *Un Ballo in Maschera* by Verdi. I attended an opera performance at least once a week—usually with a date.

While attending the wedding ceremony of a friend one night, my eyes fell upon Herta Schmidt and I came to believe in love at first sight. We danced and talked the night away, oblivious to those around us. For once I didn't resent the military government's ten o'clock curfew, because on this magical evening it meant we either had to go home early or spend the whole night at the party. We stayed. After that there was never any question of whom I would attend the theater with.

In the spring of 1946, just as Herta and I were getting serious with each other, I was called to serve a two-year mission for the Church. I was to act as a lay minister as well as help the members of the Church in my assigned area to rebuild their homes and congregation. After all the promises I had made to my Heavenly Father while in the dungeons and hell holes of the Third Reich, I felt it a great honor and a duty to provide this service and accepted the call.

I went to Herta's parents and asked for the hand of their daughter in marriage, informing them that the wedding wouldn't be until after my mission. We made the great announcement at a party the following week. As happy as I was to serve my mission, it seemed I was being separated from Herta all too soon.

After some preliminary orientations, I was asked to report to the city of Kassel, Hesse, in the central section of West Germany. The city had been ninety percent demolished by the war, which presented a real challenge to the members of the Church who lived there. My companion and I were able to go to work immediately on the task of rebuilding the congregation by seeking out our members and by teaching those who were interested in learning about the Church.

My companion happened to be the younger brother of my fiancé. Together we traveled all over the countryside in our assigned area. It was a rewarding experience and I found that the work we did in behalf of other people was a tremendous help to me in readjusting to a normal civilian life again. To paraphrase the scriptures, to find oneself, one has to lose oneself in the service of others. Many of the former camp inmates had to receive psychiatric help to readjust to life, but I felt I had found a better way.

About halfway through our mission, Herta's mother passed away. I wanted to go to Herta's side to comfort her. But since only one of us could be excused, my companion went to attend the funeral of his mother. After his return we worked very hard at our calling and had some gratifying experiences in rekindling the gospel flame among the members of the branch there. Before I knew it the two years had passed and it was time to say good-bye to my many friends in Kassel.

My love for Herta had grown even stronger during our separation, and we were both anxious to proceed with our marriage plans. The biggest problem facing us was for me to find a job that could support us. Because the war had interrupted my four-year apprenticeship, I wasn't yet qualified to work as a journeyman. I needed to work one more year as an apprentice (it should have been two, but they gave me credit for the time I worked at the airplane factory and as an assistant machinist/mechanic on Hahnoefersand Island).

I made application at the Hans Still Electric Motor Company, passed their entrance exam with flying colors, and was admitted to finish my last year. Besides making electric motors they also built electric forklifts. This factory had received an Honorable status during the war years from the Nazi Armament Commission and was considered an exclusive training facility for future journeymen of the trade. My own experience soon bore out this reputation. After about six months I ended up in the Tool & Die shop of the plant. The master Tool & Diemaker was a superb craftsman who taught me a great deal.

In the fall of 1948 something important took place in Germany. The unit of monetary exchange was still the Reichs Mark, but inflation had devalued it to the point that it was practically worthless. On a designated night the Reichs Mark was canceled and the new money, the Deutsche Mark (DM) took its place. Everyone received DM 40.00 to start out with. Credit was given for savings account balances on a ten to one ratio (10 RM = 1 DM). The effect on the economy was remarkable. Before the currency changeover, all one could find displayed in store windows were such things as cheap ashtrays made out of old artillery shells and other such junk. On the day after the exchange, the windows displayed a variety of high quality consumer goods that couldn't have been found anywhere the previous day. The good life had returned, but for awhile nobody could afford it.

On 21 January 1949, Herta and I exchanged our wedding vows. What a beautiful bride she was. At first we lived in the attic of Herta's parents' home. Our only furniture was a bed, a very small table with two chairs, and a small oven. At night the mice would run over our faces, and in the mornings our room was so cold that we often found our water bucket frozen. However, we were used to the hardships of the war years, so made the best of our situation. One night I watched my sweetheart crying while trying to start a fire in the little oven to cook dinner for us, only to have her efforts frustrated by the strong wind outside that blew the smoke back into her face. I knew she deserved better than that, so the next day I contacted the VVN, asking them to help me find an apartment. They gave me a name and a department to contact that would help us in obtaining a place of our own.

Even though the war had been over for more than three years, rationing was still in effect. This included apartment space. Apartments were assigned by a point system. Being married gave you fifty points, children counted twenty points each, victims of Nazi injustice received another fifty points, and so on. By now we were expecting our first child, which gave us twenty extra points to bargain with. I had to show my VNN card to the fellow at the desk when I turned in my application. His interest perked up immediately when he discovered that we'd been in the same concentration camp. After that my application received special handling. In what must have been a postwar bureaucratic miracle, he found an apartment for us by our next visit. He told us we could move into a one-and-a-half room apartment in Barmbeck in just a couple of weeks. Because a law had just recently passed that gave each victim of the Nazi regime a small amount of money for the time they spent in confinement, we were able to buy some furniture and live comfortably.

On 19 February 1950 our first daughter, Angelika, was born. I was so proud to be the father of such a beautiful baby. Because I had received my journeyman's papers the previous September, after passing the practical and written examinations with a B+ score, I could now afford to support the three of us. Not long after my daughter's birth I received a performance raise in pay, followed by another raise just four weeks later. I worked very hard in my trade, and my hard work didn't go unnoticed by my supervisors. Within six months I was making top wages as a Tool & Diemaker. On 22 January 1951, our second daughter, Evelyn, was born. It felt wonderful to be able to support my growing family and we were happy.

It was about this time that Herta's older brother emigrated to the United States to live in Salt Lake City, Utah. He encouraged the rest of the family to join him in America. Herta's other brother and a sister soon made the move. At the end of 1952 Herta and I were offered a chance to emigrate. In spite of some understandable fears, the anticipation and excitement built to the point that we felt we should pursue this new opportunity.

Having made the decision to emigrate, we turned our attention to the anxiety-ridden process of securing a passport and visa. First, we had to prove we were not Nazis, which was pretty easy in view of my past record. Second, we had to prove we were not Communists, which we could do because of our strong religious convictions. We then had to pass the physical examinations, take the necessary shots, and complete the mountain of paperwork. Just when we'd think we were finished, another requirement would surface. Finally the great day arrived when the mailman delivered our passports and entry visas. What excitement! It was almost scary to realize we could actually leave Germany and enter the great United States of America. Everyone admired the United States as our liberators, and it seemed like this optimistic, wealthy country would be the perfect place to raise a family.

I contacted the German/American Lines to book passage for our family and found that the earliest date we could sail was 29 May 1953 at a cost of $210.00 for each adult and one-half that amount for each of our two children. Thus, the total cost was $630.00, or 2,646 marks—a small fortune. We sold everything we could to raise the money. I even applied to the government for a settlement on my war compensation. To complete the cost of passage, my brother-in-law in Utah took out a loan, which we transferred to our name as soon as we arrived in America.

After clearing our passports and entry visas we worked frantically to get everything ready for the move. There were farewells to friends, releases from our Church assignments, a transfer of our apartment to my parents, and my last day at work. Finally everything was ready. After all this we received word that our sailing date would be delayed exactly one month because of mechanical difficulties on the ship. What a letdown! We managed to make it through the next thirty days and on 20 June 1953 set sail for America on the Italia.

The ship had a displacement of 22,000 tons and was powered by two sixteen-cylinder diesel engines. It wasn't the largest ship on the ocean, but it did carry us in comfort on our ten-day voyage to New York City. Our cabin was pleasant and the food superb. Since there were several members of our faith travelling on the same ship, we had friends to talk with and were able to hold a Sunday worship service. Our talk centered on what to expect in this strange new land that was to be our home.

The voyage went smoothly, except for one day while passing through the English Channel. The cross-current made the sea rather rough. I got so seasick, I ended up feeding the fish.

It was embarrassing enough to be the only one in our group who got seasick, but my wife couldn't resist teasing me about it. She reminded me how I had always wanted to be a sailor, and chided, "Sailors don't get seasick."After getting my sea legs, I was up and about and curious. I went to the captain and asked permission to visit the engine room. Herta stayed with the children while I went on a tour, allowing me to recover a bit of my wounded pride. While visiting the engine room I met an old school buddy of mine who was a member of the engine crew as a Machinist Mate 2nd Class. He gave me not only a royal tour of the engine room but of the whole ship. For someone who loves machines as much as I do, this was a great experience.

The voyage was a grand adventure we'll never forget. The sense of anticipation was heightened by the fact that we didn't know if we'd ever get to return to our homeland again. Our extended family seemed happy in America, and I looked forward to the chance of living in a country where freedom was an established principle of daily living. Like so many people before us, we were putting the past behind us to start our lives in the New World.

CHAPTER FOURTEEN

AMERICA

On the first of July, at five o'clock in the morning, we quietly entered New York Harbor. In spite of the early hour, I was wide awake and anxious, peering out through one of the portholes in hope of getting a view of Liberty Island. All I could see was fog. As the minutes passed, I became more and more anxious because I didn't want to miss my date with that Grand Old Lady, the Statue of Liberty. By now I had awakened the whole family and we were all pressed against the windows to get our first glimpse of the New World. Just as the ship floated by the island my prayer was answered and a ray of sunlight broke through the mist to illuminate the Statue of Liberty as she proudly welcomed us to America. Our hearts were full of gratitude. With tears in my eyes, I called my family together to kneel and give thanks to our Heavenly Father for bringing us safely to this land of promise and freedom.

As we rose from our prayer, my mind wandered back to what we had left behind in our ruined homeland. In Germany we left many of our family and friends and loved ones. We also left behind the memories of the Nazis and the war. As the sun burst forth that summer morning I felt we had a fresh start that would let us leave the past behind. I resolved to focus on the future, concentrating my energies on the life to come, not on the one we left behind. My sweet wife brought me back from my reverie by reminding me to get our things packed so we could disembark. Just then the public address system instructed us to come to the dining room to meet American Customs Officials and fill out our customs declarations. We'd planned for this in advance by making a list of all our belongings and where they were distributed in the nine different pieces of luggage that accompanied us. As I approached the Customs officer with our bags he asked where we were from. "Hamburg, Germany," I replied.

"You must be immigrants," he said.

"Yes sir," I responded. "We are going to live in the United States from now on."

"Do you have any contraband in those sea bags," he asked, smiling. I replied with an emphatic no, that it was just our personal belongings. He smiled again and waved us on, saying, "You and your family can now enter the United States. Good luck to you!" I thought that was a great welcome.

With the help of a porter, who escorted us all to the cab stand, we made our way to the Greyhound Bus terminal to begin our trip to Salt Lake City, Utah. Because of the Fourth of July holiday travellers, we had to crowd onto the bench seat in the back of the bus, which was extremely uncomfortable. Our two girls were frightened by all the strange sights and people, and wanted to sit on my wife's lap. We were miserable the next two days. The unfamiliar food combined with the heat of the summer made for an awfully uncomfortable trip. At last we arrived in Chicago where we had a layover. As we entered the cafeteria, a black waitress saw our condition and came to our rescue. We must have looked like death warmed over, so she ordered us soup, the only hot item on the menu. After some dry toast and soup we felt a little better.

Returning to the terminal we found that our bus, filled to capacity with holiday travellers, had left early. Now what? Among the people still standing were other German immigrants from the Italia. Since I spoke the best English in the group, I was elected to act as spokesman. I made my way upstairs to the terminal manager and told him there were about twenty people who wanted to go to Salt Lake City but had missed the scheduled bus through no fault of their own.

"You must all be Mormons," he said. When I answered in the affirmative he said, "So am I!" What a comfort it was to see a fellow member's face in this strange city. He picked up the phone and called down to the garage to tell them to roll out another bus for Salt Lake City. He turned to me and said, "You just go down to Station #6 and your bus will be there. Good luck and have a good life in Utah."

By now I'd learned how to slip away from the bus stops to go shopping in the side streets for groceries. Not only was the food less expensive there, but I could buy items that agreed better with our stomachs and tastes. We dined on grapes, apples, oranges, and some regular bread (meaning good, dark rye bread) for the rest of the trip. One does not change overnight what one has been used to for twenty-seven years! As my brother-in-law had said, the bus ride from New York to Salt Lake City was the price you have to pay for coming here. We found how true this was after spending four days and three nights on a crowded bus with two small children.

In spite of the difficulties, the trip was amazing. The countryside that rolled past our windows was breathtaking in its beauty. We were most surprised at the openness of the countryside. The wide open spaces were such a contrast to Germany, where everything is crowded together and people are so numerous (there are sixty times more people per square mile in Germany than in Utah).

It was about two o'clock in the afternoon when we pulled into the terminal at Salt Lake City. There, waiting patiently, were our relatives, who greeted us with open arms saying "Welcome to Salt Lake City." That night they took us to Liberty Park in the heart of Salt Lake, where the residents greeted us with fireworks and celebrations. I don't think the Fourth of July had anything to do with it.

At first, we lived as guests of my brother-in-law in his small house. After resting and talking with our relatives, we ventured out into our new world. It was such an exciting yet confusing time. An immigrant has to learn a whole new language just to get by. One of the biggest shocks was going into one of the local supermarkets. There was so much food! And, all of it had strange labels and packaging which made it difficult to get what we wanted or to know what we were getting.

The week after our arrival my brother-in-law Gerhard took a day off from work to help me find a job as a machinist. The first place we went, McGee & Hogan Machine Shop, hired me after a short interview with the shop foreman. It helped that he had a German background. In a short time I was working on a Tool & Cutter Grinder, earning a wage that could support my family. It wasn't long before we were able to afford our own apartment and furnishings. Things were going very well. It surely helped to know a trade. Even though my English wasn't very good, I was able to put my skilled hands to work right away. Usually, I could make myself understood and understand what my assignments were.

Before long I was invited to join a German thespian group. We presented a number of excellent plays to the German-speaking public of Salt Lake. I was so involved in my rehearsals that my brother-in-law had to come and get me so I could rush home to be present for the birth of our third daughter, Claudia. She was born at home and for the first time I was able to witness the birth of one of our children. What a miraculous event. That was on 30 April 1954.

On 7 December 1955 our fourth daughter Karen was born. Like her sisters, she was a beautiful baby and I was so happy that she and her mother were healthy. Three months before Karen's birth, we had signed the papers to purchase our own home. Our family complete, we were now fully settled into our community and happy in our new life in America.

In 1956 I sponsored my mother and stepfather so they could join us in our new country. What a great reunion we had when they arrived. For awhile they stayed with us, which gave the children a chance to get to know their grandparents again. They moved into their own apartment as soon as Jan found a job as a painter and my mother as a nurse's aide at a hospital. They made the adjustment to America with relative ease, and at last we were all united again.

After we had been in America for nearly five years we decided to make this our permanent home. We went to the appropriate authorities to apply for citizenship. I couldn't imagine we'd have any difficulty, but it turned out there was a problem. Some time earlier I had been approached by a co-worker at the Galigher Company, who handed me a number of leaflets that demeaned the Jews and blacks as subhumans who were unfit to be called Americans. I refused to take his leaflets and told him what I thought of his sentiments. I reminded him that this was the very line of thinking that got the Nazis started in Germany. Our discussion soon turned into an argument. He became angry and shouted, "If that's the way you feel, you must be a Communist!" This was a time in American history when anti-Communist sentiment was at a fever pitch, and many people had their careers destroyed simply because someone accused them of a Communist affiliation. I should have held my tongue, but was angry, and said, "If a feeling like mine makes one a Communist, then I must be one!"

To this he replied, "I'll get you for this!" And he did. He went to the F.B.I. and turned me in as a Communist sympathizer. Of course this threw up all kinds of red flags when it came time for my application for citizenship. I was investigated by the Bureau, who interviewed several of my friends, all of whom spoke in my behalf. In time I was given a clean bill of health, and permission was given for me to proceed with citizenship. I asked one of the investigating officers if this whole event didn't have some of the same elements of intrigue as the Nazis' system. He replied, "But, we did not lock you up and throw away the key like they did to you over there, did we?" I had to agree with him but still felt bad this incident had marred our application.

We waited for over a year before I was cleared for naturalization. I told my wife to go ahead without me, but she replied, "We came to this country together, and it will be together that we take the oath of citizenship." The time finally arrived for us to appear in the Third District Court to be sworn in as citizens. The date was 18 August 1960. We arrived an hour early to have our knowledge of the Constitution tested. We'd studied beforehand and passed with flying colors. The judge took extra time with me to make certain I was loyal. He asked some additional questions such as, "What is the difference between a totalitarian form of government and that of a democracy?" After all I'd been through, I could give a firm answer to that question. He must have liked my answers, because he said I was better prepared than most applicants and he would be honored to administer the oath of citizenship to me. We stood in the courtroom with about sixteen other people of different nationalities. Together we were sworn in as United States citizens. Then, as we repeated the Pledge of Allegiance to the flag of the United States, I found tears welling up in my eyes and felt great gratitude in my heart for the privilege I now had of being a citizen of this free country. Freedom meant a lot to me after spending so much of my youth incarcerated by the Nazis. I could proudly say, "I am an American citizen by choice, not by birth."

When I returned to work the following day the executive vice president of the company, Harold Wright, called me into his office and congratulated me on becoming a citizen, saying, "I now call you Mr. America, and I am proud of you!"

CHAPTER FIFTEEN

HONORED BY OUR HOMELAND

In the first decade following our move to America, I almost never thought about my war experiences. When dark memories surfaced I tried to put them out of my mind so they wouldn't interfere with my attitude. In 1961 I was contacted by Steve Hale, a journalist from the *Deseret News* in Salt Lake City, who heard of my experiences and wanted to write a feature article. He asked if I'd be willing to meet with him to discuss my arrest and imprisonment. I had some anxiety about our interview but tried to be as open and honest as I could. After the story appeared in the paper I was surprised to receive a number of invitations to speak at Church firesides and assemblies. I discovered that bringing my experiences out into the open made it easier to deal with the memories. It also gave me a chance to share with people the ideals and beliefs that motivated Helmuth to lead us into the Resistance. In time I would deliver my message to hundreds of audiences. There seemed to be a real interest on the part of Americans to learn about life under the Nazis.

Karl-Heinz Schnibbe had emigrated to America in 1952, nearly one year ahead of us, and had successfully established himself in the Salt Lake City community. As an excellent painter and decorator, he had no trouble finding a job with the Alfred C. Lippold Co., one of the most renowned painting establishments in the Salt Lake Valley. People were also interested to learn of his story, which included his second imprisonment in Russia as a prisoner of war.

In the mid-1970's Karl-Heinz was contacted by two professors from Brigham Young University (BYU), who were in the
process of writing a book about wartime Germany. In their research in Berlin they had obtained the original Gestapo file on
Helmuth Huebener through the American Document Center
and were interested in filling in the missing pieces of Helmuth's story by conducting in-depth interviews with those of
us who had survived.

As their work surfaced into the public, a colleague of
theirs, Dr. Thomas Rogers, decided to turn our experiences
into a play. The play, *Huebener*, premiered at BYU in October
of 1976 and ran for two weeks. My family and I saw the play
several times, but the performance that was most memorable
occurred on the last evening, when Karl-Heinz and I were
asked to stand on the stage, separated by a spotlight that illuminated a space on the floor where Helmuth would have
stood had his life not been taken by the Nazis. The audience
observed a moment of silence in memory of Helmuth, which
touched my emotions deeply.

After the play and articles appeared, I was surprised to receive a number of disturbing phone calls. I'd pick up the receiver to hear a voice say, "Landesverraeter" (traitor). It became clear to me that the underground Nazi movement, led
by German diehards, was alive and active, even in the remote
mountain deserts of Utah. Obviously, the reports of our story
touched a nerve with these people. I did not take the calls seriously or let them trouble me. Rather, I thought those who
called were either too stupid to comprehend what had happened in Germany, or they were still blinded by the simplistic
doctrines of the Nazis. In spite of these occasional sour notes,
I received even more invitations to speak about our ordeal
and was able to meet a lot of good people.

In November 1980, an article appeared in a local magazine
that again highlighted our story and told of our resistance to
the evils we saw in the Nazi regime. This alarmed a number
of people, particularly those who had embraced Nazism as a
world-saving religion, with Hitler as its divine leader. Some
of these people let us know that they still considered us to be
criminals who had broken the law.

In 1981 I had the opportunity to meet Dr. Simon Wiesen-
thal, the famous Nazi-hunter, who came to Salt Lake City as a

guest of the University of Utah. Following his speech I was invited to appear on a panel to discuss the importance of maintaining human rights as a safeguard against corrupt government.

In 1984 a local attorney wanted to produce the play *Huebener* for a Salt Lake City audience through the Walk-Ons theatre. BYU restricted the play for a time, so David Anderson, the attorney, simply wrote out his own play called *Huebener against the Reich*. The local newspapers reviewed the play, which generated a lot of interest. Karl-Heinz and I were invited to appear on local radio and television stations. The Associated Press picked up the story and passed it on to their overseas agencies. The article was translated and appeared in several German newspapers. Through this, the VVN (organization for victims of Nazi injustice) was notified of our whereabouts. They contacted me and requested a copy of the play. As I started a correspondence with the VVN, they told me several pieces of literature existed, going back as far as 1948, describing the life of Helmuth Huebener. I also learned they had been holding an annual memorial service on the date of his execution, 27 October. Soon, newspaper articles were crossing the Atlantic describing the events we participated in.

It was gratifying to learn that the City of Hamburg had not forgotten their fallen son. In 1984 the city built a beautiful youth hostel and named it the Helmuth Huebener House, complete with a memorial plaque honoring Helmuth and two other victims of the Nazi regime.

My active correspondence with the VVN culminated in an invitation for Karl-Heinz and me to return as guests of the Hamburg State Senate to visit the city for a memorial service to be held in Helmuth's honor on 8 January 1985—what would have been his sixtieth birthday. The City of Hamburg offered to pay all our expenses. We were excited, and immediately agreed to make the trip. Since it would be our first visit back to our homeland, both Karl-Heinz and I decided to lengthen the visit by an extra week so we could visit family and friends.

It was cold when we arrived at the Hamburg Airport, but we received a warm and enthusiastic welcome from our relatives and the official representatives of the Hamburg Senate. Our wives received a big bouquet of flowers from both the

City of Hamburg and the Presidium of the VVN. Their hands were full, our eyes were wide, and my heart raced at being back in Germany. Cars swiftly took us to the Hotel Vorbach, where we dropped into bed, exhausted. One caller awakened us in the middle of our sleep just to welcome us to the city, not realizing we were suffering from jet lag. The next morning we were rested enough to eat a good Hamburg breakfast of boiled eggs and freshly baked hard rolls.

At 10:30 A.M. on Monday our hosts took us on a tour of Glasmoor prison. Dr Alan Keele, one of the BYU professors who had been instrumental in bringing our story to light, joined us there for the tour. What bittersweet memories we encountered while touring the old prison. It is still in use today but conditions are much different than they were in the 1940s. Karl-Heinz said, "This is more like a recreational spa than a prison!" I agreed there were a lot of changes. Thank heavens, too, for no one should suffer the treatment that the prisoners of Glasmoor received at the hands of the Nazis.

Our next stop was the former concentration camp in Fuhlsbuettel, KOLAFU, Suhrenkamp 98. The VVN invited us to place a large bouquet of flowers at the gate of the camp in memory of the victims who had suffered there. Standing in front of the gate brought a flashback of the day I went through the gate to be greeted by the Lange Paul, who started to kick and beat me. I remembered the stranger who pushed me against the wall, shielding my body with his as he said, "Disappear into the wall." For forty-three years I had so effectively pushed this and other tortures from my mind that I couldn't even remember my protectors name. As I stood there in front of the gate it finally came to me that his name was Hans. At that I broke down and cried and said a silent, "Thank you, Hans, for my life." After awhile I got my composure back and noticed people looking at me, but I had the feeling they understood, since they were the kind of people who still remember and honor victims of Nazi oppression.

I didn't much enjoy the tour of KOLAFU. The memories were too real and painful. We consumed a light lunch there, but I didn't have much of an appetite.

Our next stop was the Hamburg Investigative Prison where we joined the Presidium of the VVN in placing flowers in front of a memorial plaque honoring the Christian Clergy of the City of Luebeck who had been executed for their beliefs. We were escorted through the halls of the prison for some additional memories. It was here we had listened to the cries of the soon-to-be-executed prisoners as they faced the 5:00 A.M. moment of death. The executions took place every day but Sunday. I was glad when the time came to leave this place, feeling somehow as if the walls were closing in on me. I asked Karl-Heinz how he was doing, and he told me he was feeling depressed too.

That night we attended a program at the Helmuth Huebener Memorial Assembly Hall at the new Helmuth Huebener House in the St. Pauli section of Hamburg. Behind the speaker's forum hung an oversize picture of Helmuth, a picture of the Three Musketeers (Karl-Heinz, Helmuth, and me at ages seventeen, sixteen, and fifteen), and an oversized copy of the public bulletin that announced the execution of Helmuth for treason against the Reich. There were other placards stating, "Never Again Fascism," "No More War," and "No More Nuclear Missiles."The program featured remarks by various speakers highlighting Helmuth's resistance, including quotes from his handbills, excerpts from the trial, his mother's appeal for clemency, and even the recommendation of clemency from the Gestapo. Karl-Heinz and I were both invited to speak. Shortly before giving my remarks, the president of the VVN leaned over and whispered into my ear, "Perhaps you could remark about the judgment of the 'Peoples Court,' and allude to the fact that it is still in effect."

The VVN had been working with the government to have the judgments of the court set aside permanently, both to exonerate its victims and to officially wipe away the stain it left on German history. In my remarks I denounced the Volksgerichtshof, as an unlawful tool of the Nazi dictatorship that had been created for the sole purpose of eliminating opposition to the party and to terrorize the German people. I went on to say it had ruled by fear and made capricious judgments having no legal foundations whatsoever. I finished with a well received call to the Bundestag (German Parliament) to declare the judgments passed by the infamous Volksgerictshof as illegal, null and void, and to identify it as a criminal Nazi institution. (In the fall of that year the Bundestag passed legislation to that effect.)

The following day, Tuesday, 8 January, we went to the School for Administration where the official memorial service for Helmuth's sixtieth birthday was arranged. The school's assembly hall was named for Helmuth, since this was the school he had attended. After a musical tribute, the Director for the Governmental Office of Rehabilitation & Social Services gave a talk outlining the meaning of democracy and commended the heroic role and example Helmuth Huebener had set for the students who were now attending the school. Karl-Heinz and I gave a report of the resistance work carried out by our little band, and our part in it. I used several quotes from Helmuth's beloved authors such as Klaus Bonhoeffer who said, "Evil should be smothered right from the beginning," and quotes from the Bible's Book of Revelation that said, "And he opened his mouth in blasphemy against God, to Blaspheme His name" (Revelation 13: 5–6). Helmuth believed this description fit Hitler perfectly. I then described the kind of God Helmuth believed in, a God of kindness and peace. Our messages were well received by those who attended.

On Wednesday we were invited to an official reception in the Senate wine cellar of the Hamburg State Senate. In addition to the senators, other high dignitaries from the political parties, newspaper editors, and businessmen were in attendance. I sat next to the president of the Senate and had an enjoyable conversation with him that ended in an invitation for him to visit us in Salt Lake City when he next came to America. Senator Jan Ehlers welcomed us as host and paid tribute to the events of four decades earlier. We told the group how grateful we were for the invitation to come to Hamburg, our native home. We were treated like royalty that day, culminating in a visit to the opera house for a performance of Mozart's *Cosi fan tutte*.

On Thursday, 10 January, we went to the Neuengamme concentration camp on the Elbe. From 1938 until 1945 a total of 106,000 people were imprisoned there—55,000 of them lost their lives there. Even though he wasn't part of the official statistics, our friend Heinrich Worbs was one of Neuengamme's victims, because he died so shortly after his imprisonment for speaking against the "Nazi butchers." In addition to the main camp, Neuengamme had over sixty auxiliary camps that provided slave labor to the industrial complexes nearby.

Friday was to conclude our official visit with a trip to Hah-noefersand Island. Unfortunately, Karl-Heinz had the flu, so only his wife could attend. I was surprised to find the prison now accessible by a land bridge that extended out into the Elbe River. In the last days of the war the island could only be reached by boat. I actually had some pleasant memories of this place, particularly when I saw the old water tower from which I had watched the advance of the Allies.

The camp was still in use for youth offenders, and I had the chance to speak to them about my experiences there, including the day I almost lost my life after telling the Nazi recruiter I would not join the army. I was pleasantly surprised to see the humane treatment afforded prisoners in this modern camp.

That night we attended a final dinner and reception of the VVN, where we had the chance to tell about our life in America and visit with the members. Then came a big surprise. The president of the VVN stood and told us we had been awarded the Medal of Honor of the VVN, "For outstanding merits in the fight against the National Socialistic tyranny, and the reestablishment of freedom and democracy." It was signed by Dr. J.C. Rossaint, national president of the VVN. He had been accused at a 1937 trial against the German Catholic clergy, who had been vocal in the fight against Nazism. For his efforts the People's Court sentenced him to eleven years in the penitentiary, with the deprivation of human rights for an additional ten years after release. He spent eight years behind bars.

I was touched to receive the award. In 1942 we were branded traitors. Four decades later we were being honored as heroes. It was wonderful to be in a new Germany where men of conscience once again held power. I was honored to rub shoulders with so many who had been courageous in opposing tyranny. With the official visit ended, we took time to visit relatives and friends throughout Germany.

On the following Wednesday we took a flight from Hamburg to Berlin. There, with Karl-Heinz and his wife, we crossed the border into East Berlin. The guards at the border were very strict, but Karl-Heinz worked some of his old organizational magic, and the way was soon open to us.

In East Berlin we were guests of the highly respected writer, Stephan Hermlin, who has written several books on the Resistance movement. Hermlin had used Helmuth as a character in one of his books. He wrote, "There are times and places where children do not dream any more about how to commit pranks, but about how to take the government to task." We had a delightful visit with Dr. Hermlin and his Russian wife. At the conclusion of the visit, he presented me a copy of his book, *The First Line*, which he endorsed, "To Rudolf Wobbe, in friendship and with respect. Stephan Hermlin, 17 January 1985." I was thrilled to receive this gracious gift. As we made our way back toward West Berlin I noticed how drab East Berlin looked. Many of the old bombed out buildings remained, even after forty years. People drove old cars and stood in lines to purchase food. The contrast was vivid. Democracy certainly provides a more abundant life for its citizens.

Before we knew it, the time arrived for us to leave. The trip, with all its events and receptions, had been the thrill of my life. We were honored to be received by the great men and women of the VVN.

Probably the worst event of the trip was a visit we made to the execution chamber where Helmuth was beheaded. To reach this awful place, one has to travel down a long road lined by dark, towering trees on one side and the tall, foreboding walls of the prison on the other. As we entered the chamber, there was such a presence of evil and death that I felt tightness in my chest so severe I could hardly breathe. My wife had a similar feeling of oppression, and, literally shaking, we both made our way outside to escape the awful feeling. I felt a stab of sorrow for Helmuth, who had to walk into that room as a teenager, all alone to face death. But, Helmuth had great confidence he would be received by a God who knew his heart and loved him. Of that I have no doubt.

Epilogue

In my mind, I still remember the happy days when Helmuth and I walked through the spring evenings, singing songs, talking of life, and committing ourselves to freedom. For us, the great dilemma had been that we were raised in a closed society that crushed freedom of speech and expression. Yet, through the influence of our Christian upbringing we had come to believe in the freedom of the individual and the obligation of good men to support truth. We resisted our government and broke a law by listening to the BBC. The People's Court ruled that we committed the crime of Preparation to High Treason by taking the information thus gained to our neighbors through handbills and leaflets.

I take comfort from a statement by Kurt Huber, the intellectual head of the White Rose movement, who was executed on 13 July 1943. He said,

> There is a point at which the law becomes immoral and unethical. That point is reached when it becomes a cloak for the cowardice that dares not stand up against blatant violations of justice. A state that suppresses all freedom of speech and which, by imposing the most terrible punishment, treats each and every attempt at criticism, however morally justified, and every suggestion for improvement as "plotting to high treason," is a state that breaks an unwritten law.

I believe that unwritten law is a law of God declaring that all men are to have free agency, to act according to their conscience. Looking back across time I see so many brave men and women who stood up in the fight against Nazism. Strong in their opposition were the priests and ministers of many of the churches in the land. In February of 1985, Karl-Heinz and I received an invitation to attend a reception of the Utah Chapter of the Freedom Foundation at Valley Forge, to be cited in their We Believe in Heroes program. In a wonderful event in the Grand Ballroom of the Little America hotel, we received a plaque and a handshake from Utah's Governor, Norman Bangerter. Now, our efforts had been recognized in both our native and adopted hometowns. It is a privilege to live in a land of freedom.

President Ezra Taft Benson, former United States Secretary of Agriculture and now President of the Church, said in a speech entitled, "A Moral Challenge," "I say to you with all the fervor of my soul that God intended men to be free. Rebellion against tyranny is a righteous cause." What an honor it was to know a man like Helmuth Huebener and to have joined with him and the others in resisting the tyranny that gripped the land of our birth.

AFTERWORD

On 24 January 1992, Rudi and I signed the publishing agreement that made this book possible. He said it was one of the greatest days of his life. The moment was poignant because Rudi had contracted cancer nearly half a year earlier. Major surgery had removed most of the cancer, but the radiation treatment made it difficult for the wound to heal. That day, chemotherapy left him looking tired and drawn—not at all the way he was during the three years that we worked together on the manuscript. Rudi always had a fresh scrubbed look, with his hair neatly combed, and his eyes sparkling. It was difficult for him to settle down to the task of recovering from a disease that he couldn't "shake off" in just a few days. While battling cancer, Rudi never lost his vigor, or his positive attitude. While being wheeled to the operating table, he was busily telling the doctors and nurses about his experiences, and encouraging them to read his story when it was published. On 31 January 1992, one week after signing our agreement, Rudi Wobbe passed away.

A violent storm raged outside the church in Rothenbergsort on the day in 1926 when Rudi was christened. As the priest took Rudi in his arms, a loud thunderclap rocked the old chapel, which inspired the priest to nickname Rudi, "Boy of Thunder!" Prophetic words, indeed. Never one to hurt another person, Rudi stood up firmly and unfailingly for what he believed to be true. Regardless of the consequences, he spoke his mind and was honest and courageous to the end. He was a great friend, father, and husband—we all miss him.

Rudi Wobbe   Jerry Borrowman

About the Author

Dave Kadleck, Rudi Wobbe's son-in-law introduced Rudi and Jerry. It took just a few minutes with Rudi Wobbe to convince Jerry that the compelling experiences he had to share could easily fill a book. After deciding they could work together, they began the task of organizing the story into an outline for the manuscript. Jerry listened intently to the fascinating story of Rudi's youth and his fierce devotion to a boyhood friend, Helmuth Huebener. Rudi had an uncanny ability at organization and expression, providing phrases that evoked an immediate visual response. They worked together on the book for three years.

Jerry said, "For the rest of my life I'll remember hearing Rudi's optimistic, 'Well hello, Jerry.' His German accent gave an unusual lilt to the words, and no matter how discouraging the moment, I always felt brighter after meeting with him. Prompt and punctual, opinionated yet courteous, he won my heart."

Their wives Herta and Marcella played a crucial role in the manuscript. Herta helped Rudi decide what should and shouldn't be included, while Marcella proved to be an outstanding editor. It's our hope that all who read this book will be encouraged by the strength of Rudi's convictions and that we will each stand with the same courage he displayed, when life challenges us to defend truth and freedom.

This book details the story of Rudi's life. He passed away in January 1992. Jerry Borrowman works as a training consultant for the New York Life Insurance company in Salt Lake City, Utah. A political science graduate of Idaho State University, he's had numerous articles published in the *Ensign*, the *Review*, and other periodicals. This is his first book. He and Marcella are the parents of three sons and a daughter.